MARQUE SPOTLIGHT SERIES NUMBER THIRTEEN

MG DOWNUNDER

Original text written and researched
by Barry Lake
Editor–at–Large
MOTOR Magazine

THE MARQUE SPOTLIGHT SERIES with ROADTESTS FROM MOTOR
is a unique series with a strong Australian accent. It highlights interesting individual
car models (and model series) by providing information, specifications, photographs
and contemporary material, including roadtests. It is aimed at owners, potential
owners and enthusiasts alike.

MARQUE
PUBLISHING COMPANY

MARQUE SPOTLIGHT SERIES NUMBER THIRTEEN
MG DOWNUNDER

Original text written and researched by Barry Lake with additional material by Peter Kerr.
© Copyright 1994: Marque Publishing Company Pty Ltd.

First published in 1994 by Marque Publishing Company Pty Ltd, 911 King Georges Road Blakehurst 2221
(PO Box 203 Hurstville 2220). Phone (02) 546 5521.

National Library of Australia:
ISBN 0 947079 41 6

Design by Tracy Gilholme.
Production by Tracy Gilholme and Tony Davis.
Typesetting and assembly by Type Forty, Glebe.
Printed in Australia by Ligare Pty Ltd.

The author and publishers would like to especially thank Peter Kerr and Graham Howard for their assistance during the preparation of this manuscript.

Photo sources: Automotive News Service, Marque Publishing Company, Royal Automobile Club of Australia, MOTOR magazine (nee Modern Motor) and Australian Motor Sports magazine.

Marque Publishing Company would like to thank the following for assistance, advice and sympathy: David Robertson, Adrian McComb, John Thornley, Pip Bucknell, Andrew Quinn, the RAC and the publishers of Australia's leading monthly automotive magazine, MOTOR (nee Modern Motor), who have kindly allowed Marque to reproduce historic road–tests.

CONTENTS

SPECIAL NOTE ON POWER OUTPUT AND SPECIFICATIONS:

Variance may be found in specifications, particularly in power output figures, due to different methods used for measuring. Except where otherwise stated, the specifications given in the text for individual model cars are those issued by the manufacturer at the time each vehicle was released.

Unfortunately different systems of measuring power have been used in Australia at various times and each system produces a different figure for the same engine.

In the early days of motoring, the most commonly used unit was the horsepower. The lack of an agreed method for measuring horsepower, however, led to the widespread use of an artificial system. This was instituted by the British Royal Automobile Club and involved a formula which included the bore diameter and the number of cylinders. It was expressed in rated horsepower (HP). As engine technology improved, this rating became less accurate, giving figures well below the actual power output, but the system was still widely used, particularly by governments for taxation purposes. Even in the 1970s and early 1980s, some car companies published the rated HP figures for their engines as well as the actual output. Where possible we have included these figures.

To gain a more valid guide to engine power, the system of measuring 'brake horsepower' using an engine dynamometer came into fashion. From the 1940s, the US system of measuring 'SAE brake horsepower' was widely used here. These figures (derived from test procedures developed by the Society of Automotive Engineers) provide the gross power of an engine without the exhaust system and some ancillary equipment fitted. The results were flattering (and became even more so as the companies found new ways to fudge the numbers). In the 1970s, a trend developed towards issuing net horsepower figures, measured with most or all of the engine equipment attached. Different methods still produced different 'net' results, but since 1976 when Australia adopted the SI Metric system, the situation has improved. From 1976 all figures were measured in kilowatts, with 75kW being approximately equal to 100bhp. The industry also started to change to 'installed power' which is based on an Australian standard similar to the German DIN system.

As a result, the quoted power figures are less flattering but more accurate and comparable. In 1969, for example, Holden claimed 300bhp for its top–line 1969 Monaro but in 1988 the company claimed only 180kW (240bhp) for its more powerful fuel–injected 'Group A' V8. Ford Australia's figures took a similar tumble.

For the Marque Spotlight Series, we have converted all figures (except rated horsepower) to kiloWatts and, as a general rule, you can assume that figures are 'gross' up to the mid–1970s, then 'net' until the late 1970s/early 1980s, when 'installed' figures became almost universal.

Performance figures too are subject to conjecture but we have endeavoured to check with as many sources as possible and give what we believe to be the best available guide to the performance of each car when new.

ABOUT THE AUTHOR

Barry Lake became hooked on motoring and motor racing as an eight–year–old boy, in 1951, when his father began working in the motor industry and first took him to the Bathurst Easter race meeting that year. At 14 years of age he bought his first car, by age 18 he was working for a motor auction company. He bought his first race car, a Cooper–Norton Mark V, in 1961. Throughout the 1960s Lake raced the Cooper, and further open–wheel racing cars to outright victory at Warwick Farm and Oran Park, class wins at Catalina Park, and a second outright at Bathurst.

Lake drove a service car on the Australian section of the 1968 London–Sydney Marathon, and in 1969 began rally driving with Mitsubishi. Driving Colts through 1969–70–71, he led the Mitsubishi team to win the Teams Award in the 1970 KLG International Rally of The Hills. Lake also began navigating in rallies and directing championship rally events. In 1972 he navigated Brian Hilton's Peugeot 504 to second place in the NSW Rally Championship, and was a regular visitor to New Caledonia for that country's Safari during the 1970s.

Lake's writing career started with rally reports for Australian Motoring News in 1970 and he soon became Rally Editor, then Assistant Editor of that publication. He left to join Racing Car News as Assistant Editor, then moved on to become founding Editor of Chequered Flag magazine. In 1977 he joined Off Road Australia and moved to Modern MOTOR (now MOTOR) in 1979. He was Editor of Modern MOTOR from 1981 to 1989, since which time he has worked from home as Editor–at–Large for the same magazine. From his earliest writing days, Lake has contributed stories to publications in England and Japan. Motoring writing has led to Lake road–testing most cars on the Australian market during the past 23 years, as well as track–testing many competition cars, and riding on circuits and rally stages with some of Australia's and the world's best race and rally drivers.

A class win and an outright 6th placing in the Southern Cross International Rallies of 1973–74–75 marked three years with Subaru, and Lake raced BMWs in the Hardie–Ferodo 1000 at Bathurst in 1976 and 1978. In 1977 he competed in the Singapore Airlines London–Sydney Marathon with Brian Hilton in a Peugeot 504, running as high as fourth outright before mechanical problems dropped them back in the field.

The 1979 Repco Round Australia Trial saw Lake sharing a Marlboro–Holden Dealer Team Holden Commodore with international stars Rauno Aaltonen and Shekhar Mehta to place third outright in the famous Holden 1–2–3 clean sweep of the event.

A factory–backed Subaru was Lake's mount in the original Australian (Wynn's) Safari in 1985, followed by a works Mitsubishi in 1986. In 1988 Lake finished second in class in the Australian Motorkhana Championship and won the Group 7 Sports Drivers' Championship the same year. Also in 1988, he flew to Japan three times, for the last two rounds of the All–Japan Sports Car Championship as Team Manager for the Team Schuppan Rothmans Porsche 962, and as an assistant with the factory Porsche team entry in the Fuji round of the 1988 World Sports Car Championship.

Late in 1990 Lake navigated Denis Hulme to place third outright in the Lucas Grand Prix Rally in a Mercedes–Benz 500SL. In 1992 he was fifth in the inaugural Targa Tasmania with Sir Jack Brabham in a Honda NS–X, and competed with Alan Hamilton in a Porsche Carrera 2 in the Dutton Grand Prix Rally. The big event for 1993 was the Lombard London–Sydney Marathon in which he co–drove a Ford Falcon GT with Ian Vaughan to second place outright in the 30–day, 15,700km event.

Lake has also been an advanced driving instructor since the mid–1970s, with schools owned by Peter Wherrett, Ian Luff, and Peter Finlay, as well as assisting Finnish ace Rauno Aaltonen with schools in 1979 and 1991.

Lake has contributed to many magazines and books, particularly as a consultant on a number of motor racing histories. His 'Spotlight on Brock Commodore' was published by Marque in 1992.

TITLE PAGE: In sales terms, the MGB was the most successful of them all. Well over half a million were made, including several thousand assembled at the plant owned by the British Motor Corporation (later British Leyland, then Leyland Australia) at Zetland, NSW.
COVER (Clockwise from top left): (a) Peter Kerr, of Nambour, Queensland, competes regularly in his concours–winning 1935 supercharged N–type Magnette. (photo by R&M Motor Racing.) (b) Ian Heather Jnr's 1929 M–type Midget with a single overhead cam, 847 cc engine. (c) A fine example of the very successful MGB, photographed soon after it was restored by Dr Gerard Tester of Sydney during the 1980s.(d) Ed Holly's 1959 MGA coupe shows its pace during an historic motor race at Eastern Creek, NSW, in September 1993.

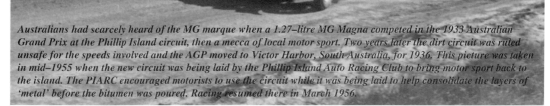

Australians had scarcely heard of the MG marque when a 1.27–litre MG Magna competed in the 1933 Australian Grand Prix at the Phillip Island circuit, then a mecca of local motor sport. Two years later the dirt circuit was ruled unsafe for the speeds involved and the AGP moved to Victor Harbor, South Australia, for 1936. This picture was taken in mid–1955 when the new circuit was being laid by the Phillip Island Auto Racing Club to bring motor sport back to the island. The PIARC encouraged motorists to use the circuit while it was being laid to help consolidate the layers of 'metal' before the bitumen was poured. Racing resumed there in March 1956.

'Old No. 1', the original MG sports two–seater. It was not the first car called MG, but the first purpose–built model, as the earlier MGs had been lightly modified Bullnose Morris tourers with special bodywork. This car — considered the first real MG — was built for managing director Cecil Kimber. Completed in March 1925, it had the 48th body built by Carbodies of Coventry for Morris Garages, Oxford. Kimber and 'Old Number 1' won a gold medal in the Land's End Trial in Easter that year.

The men who made the marque. Chief Executive Cecil Kimber and proprietor Sir William Morris on their way to lunch. The occasion was the opening of the new MG factory — established in a former leather works in Abingdon, Oxfordshire, in early 1930. At that time Sir William owned MG (Morris Garages) privately but the mechanical components were bought from Morris Motors Ltd, a public company.

As production gets into full swing, a batch of M–type Midgets leaves the factory in 1930. A few 'Sportsman's Coupes' can be seen in the background.

MG DOWNUNDER

MG BEGINNINGS

The story of MG cars in their early years is very much the story of the car's creator, Cecil Kimber, the man who in his determination to build an affordable sports car that was fun to drive, created the MG marque. After working in other areas of the motor industry, including the original Aston Martin company, Kimber was appointed to the position of sales manager for Morris Garages, the sales arm of the William Morris–owned Morris Motors Ltd, in 1921. Only a year later Kimber became general manager when the former GM left abruptly and then committed suicide. Kimber dabbled in body design as well as managing the company, at a time when it was common for cars to be sold in chassis form and fitted with bodies by various coach–building companies to the customer's choice. Kimber was able to boost the profits on mundane Morris Cowleys by converting them into far more desirable machines with special bodywork and other options. He was in the 1920s, to Morris cars what Peter Brock was to become to Holdens in Australia in the 1980s.

Before long another separate company was formed — the MG Car Company (the MG initials derived from 'Morris Garages') — for the purpose of building special cars based on the original Morris creations. Pinning down Kimber's first MG model, however, has eluded most historians. The world's most noted chronicler of the MG story, F. Wilson McComb, has written that this is because there wasn't really one particular car that first bore the MG name. Rather, there was a long line of modified Morris models that eventually evolved into the MG sports car.

The first MG built in any real numbers was the 14/28 Super Sports, released in 1924. It was based on the famous 'bull–nose' Morris Cowley and shared that car's distinctive radiator shape. Some 400 of these were built and sold before the appearance of the 'flat radiator' 14/28 and the 14/40 which followed in the years 1926 to 1929. This new flat–fronted look was to develop into the familiar MG radiator shape for the 18/80 Six released in 1928. The basic radiator/grille shape remained (in a forever evolving form), until the 1955 MG TF. There-

after it had to be greatly modified for the lower, aerodynamic MGA, and the even later MGB and its derivatives but it was still recognisable.

MG cars were to change the way motoring enthusiasts were to think and feel about sports cars, driving, and motor sport. Although there were some highly specialised and expensive racing and racing–sports cars from the company over the years, as well as a few quite luxurious — and equally expensive — saloons, the name MG to most people conjures up visions of small, simple, light weight and relatively inexpensive sports cars that were fun to drive and surprisingly quick from point to point. The epitome of this image was the MG Midget in its various guises, which thrilled and delighted enthusiast drivers for more than 50 years, from the late–1920s to the end of the 1970s.

Since this book is primarily about the MG car in Australia, and since the marque did not become at all common on our roads until the mid–1930s, we shall not dwell on the early company history. This has, in fact, been dealt with thoroughly in numerous publications. All of the major models are listed elsewhere in this book.

MG IN AUSTRALIA

Exactly when the first MG came to Australia is a question that hasn't been satisfactorily answered in recent times. For such a popular marque and one which has been well docu-

CHRONOLOGY

1877: William Morris, son of a farmer, is born at Worcester.
1904: William Morris starts 'Morris Garages' in Oxford.
1921: Cecil Kimber joins Morris as sales manager.
1921: Syd Enever (later MG's chief engineer) joins Morris Garages as errand boy.
1922: Kimber appointed general manager of Morris.
1923: George Harriman (later chairman of BMC) joins Morris.
1924: MG Bullnose Morris released.
1925: 'Old Number One' becomes the first entirely special purpose–built MG sports car. Made for Kimber's own use. Kimber enters the car in the Land's End Trial and wins a gold medal. Production of MGs moves to Morris Radiators Branch factory in Bainton Rd, Oxford, from previous sites at Longwall and Alfred Lane.

mented in England, it is surprising that the early history of MGs in Australia is decidedly vague.

As recently as 1980, Sydney motoring historian David Manson wrote on this very subject in the VSCCA's magazine called 'Vintage Car'. Manson said that in 1960 Mr Stan Hill, who had been Sales Manager of Williams Brothers from 1921 to 1925, when that company was an agent for Morris, Sunbeam and Alvis cars, sent him a photo of a proud family posing with their car — claimed to be one of the early bull–nosed MG 14/28 cars. Since cars were usually shipped to Australia in those days in chassis form, to have bodies built upon them locally, it is not surprising that the car shown has a body different, not only from English MG 14/28s, but also from the Morris Oxford 14/28 on which that first MG was based. Manson sent a copy of the photo to Morris historian Lytton Jarman, who said it had the right wheels to be an MG, but the non–standard body made it otherwise impossible to tell if the car was a Morris or an MG. He did confirm that it was definitely of 1925 or earlier vintage.

Williams Brothers, around that time, ran a team of Alvis 12/50 'Duck's Back' models in various motor sport events, and also imported the Alvis with which Phil Garlick became famous for his exploits at Maroubra Speedway, as well as the Grand Prix Sunbeam raced by Hope Bartlett. It would be reasonable to assume that such enthusiastic motor sales people would have been keen enough to import one of the new MGs, or to have modified a Morris to similar specifications. The car just might have been our first MG, or at least was a very reasonable copy of one. Stan Hill said the car was run at Penrith Speedway in the 1920s but ran its bearings on the first lap.

It is also interesting to note that the sons of Williams Brothers started the company P & R Williams which was, in later years, a major MG dealer in NSW.

David Manson also recollects that the oldest MG he ever saw in Australia was '...a very nice square nose tourer, perhaps a 14/40 of about 1928. This was around the Chatswood area quite a lot in the late 1940s'.

Ian Heather (Jnr) of Blaxland in NSW, in 1964, bought a 1929 MG M–type (the original MG Midget, built from 1929 to 1932 by Morris Garages in England) in poor condition and without its body, which he believed had been imported to Australia new. Heather restored the car and fitted a replica body — suggesting the car was probably imported in chassis form and fitted with a local body, as there were extra duties imposed on cars with bodies in those days.

Heather also suggested — in information offered for a book on vintage cars produced some years ago by the publishers of this book — that very few MGs were imported around that time.

Further clues to early imports of MGs can be garnered by studying the racing career of Les Jennings, a stalwart of the early Australian GPs. Jennings was a salesman at Lane's Motors (later a prominent MG dealer and still selling cars in Melbourne today) which at the time sold Morris cars. Jennings drove a 1550cc Morris Cowley, stripped of its mudguards, in the first ever Australian Grand Prix, at Phillip Island (Vic) on 26 March 1928, retiring from the event. Jennings missed the 1929 AGP, but was back in 1930 with an 847cc Morris Minor — the model on which the very first MG Midget, the M–type, was based — only to retire again. Unsuccessful again in 1931 with an 1802cc Morris Oxford, Jennings finally managed to finish the AGP in 1932, in 7th place, with a 1548cc Morris Cowley.

CHRONOLOGY

1926: Success of MG prompts the opening of a separate factory at Edmund Road, Oxford, in September.

1927: MG Car Company formed with Sir William Morris as governing director and Cecil Kimber as managing director. Morris takes over Wolseley. MG Bullnoses discontinued. MG 14/28 (later 14/40 Mark IV) released in GB. The 14/28 (14/40) was the first MG to bear the brown and beige octagon MG badge and the first MG to be exhibited at a Motor Show (London). In October a 14/40 becomes the first MG to win a motor racing event, in Buenos Aires.

1928: MG 18/80 MkI and MkII released. MG 18/80 Mark I is the first chassis of MG's own design and the first MG to bear the Kimber designed radiator.

1929: MG factory begins moving to disused part of Pavlova leather works at Abingdon–on–Thames, south of Oxford. All MGs were then built there. MG 14/40 Mark IV discontinued. MG M–type Midget released.

1930: MG 18/100 Mark III 'Tigress' released. Donald Stokes (later Chairman British Leyland) joins Leyland Motors.

Lane's Motors, and Jennings, must surely have been interested in importing and racing the new MG marque during those years. That they appear not to have done so suggests either that MG cars were selling so well in Britain they were unavailable for export in numbers, or that Lane's could not yet see a market for such a car, or perhaps that they intended to concentrate on racing — and thereby promoting — the greater–volume selling Morris models.

AUSTRALIA'S FIRST RACING MG

By March 1933, however, an MG Magna F–type had been brought into the country, a model which was built in England in 1931 and 1932 and was the fastest MG to that time. The F–type Magna had an engine similar in design to that in the little M–type, but with six cylinders instead of four, to give a capacity of 1271cc. Power claimed was 37.2bhp (27.8kW) at 4100rpm. It had a four–speed non–synchromesh gearbox and 'knock–on' wire wheels as were to become synonymous with MG sports cars for the rest of their days with only occasional exceptions. This car has been reported in some areas as having been imported by Lane's Motors, although Les Jennings' family years later maintained that it was brought in privately.

The two–seater F–type set the style for MG sports cars, a shape which was to be developed all the way through to the 1955 MG TF, the last of the 'square riggers'. Jennings' Australian–bodied (by Aspinal) MG for the 1933 AGP, though, was stripped of its full–width windscreen (replaced by two small 'aero' screens for him and his riding mechanic), lighting equipment, bonnet sides, and mudguards. Even though the AGP at that time was still run from a handicap start, Jennings' MG, which he is said to have prepared himself, ran to a fast and reliable third outright behind Bill Thompson's Brooklands Riley and Harold Drake–Richmond's Bugatti Type 37.

Jennings' MG obviously caused quite a stir at the time, because Neil Gullifer, who raced a Ballot in that 1933 Grand Prix and was a director of Britannia Motors, immediately began machinations aimed at grabbing the MG agency from Lane's Motors. He failed, and Lane's went on to become one of the largest MG dealers in the country.

Lending further credence to our assumed dearth of MGs prior to 1933, is a story in 'The Motor in Australia and Flying', written by J O Sherwood and dated 1 December 1933. Sherwood was later to win the 150–Mile race at Bathurst in 1939 in an MG NE Magnette and, after the war, was the long–standing promoter of the Speedway Royale at the Sydney RAS Showgrounds.

Sherwood wrote: '...The MG has until recently been only a sort of myth in the minds of local car enthusiasts... for some surprising reason these cars have not been represented on the Australian market, and their wonderful performances could only be read of and wondered at, but not actually demonstrated in the flesh. It was therefore with great and unusual interest that the test of the latest MG — stocks of which are now available to the Australian public — was carried out'.

Unfortunately there is no explanation of how or why this situation had changed, nor mention of who supplied the car tested.

Of the car, a J2 Midget (these were manufactured in England between 1932 and 1934), Sherwood wrote: '... a piquant and intensely alive little car... the road is no longer a highway from place to place, but a path of adventure... This modern four–cylinder 847cc engine in the MG J2 is of fine design and it runs with notable smoothness ... from a comfortable toddle on top gear right up to over 5000 revs per minute when all out... one cannot but be impressed with the absolutely remarkable all round ability of the car..'.

Photographs show the tested J2 had arrived in chassis form, with radiator, bonnet and headlamps, but no other bodywork. Sherwood can be seen sitting low behind the windscreen–less cowl on an extremely low–mounted driving seat. Time quoted for the standing start quarter mile is 19.4 seconds, petrol consumption achieved was 45mpg, and the top speed attained was quoted as 83mph.

As already mentioned, Robert T. Lane was to become an enthusiastic distributor of MG cars, as well as owning and driving examples of the marque himself. In 1934 Lane brought into the country a K3 Magnette model MG and employed Australia's then–fastest racing driver, Bill Thompson, to race it. Thompson was also given the position of Manager of Lanes Motors' MG Division and a secondary task of 'Test Driver'.

The K3 Magnette had been introduced early in 1933 and had been designed specifically for competition use. A team of K3s ran in the Mille Miglia in Italy that year, finishing first and second in the under 1100cc class. Later the same year, the great Tazio Nuvolari drove one of the works cars to outright victory in the Ulster Tourist Trophy at Ards. The Lane car had been driven by Tim Birkin and expatriate Australian Bernard Rubin in the Mille Miglia, but retired. It competed in a few more events with different drivers before being sent to Australia.

In the Australian GP at Phillip Island in March 1934 Bill Thompson, who'd already won three AGPs (two with Bugattis and one with a Riley), set fastest race lap and fastest overall time, but failed by only 24 seconds to catch the winning Singer of Bob Lea–Wright, which had started an incredible 35 minutes ahead of him!

AUSTRALIAN BODIES ON MGs

In the pre–war days of British Empire trade preferences, the strongest export markets for Morris and Austin vehicles were Australia and South Africa. The Australian government, for its part, was anxious to nurture its own motor industry, and import duties on bodywork were introduced as early as 1907. This was followed by duties on chassis and other components in 1920.

However, with the Empire Trade Preference scheme, unassembled chassis of British origin could be imported duty–free and most of the MGs came over in this form. They were also advertised in the MG export sales brochures as a distinct item. For example, in the 1935 export sales brochure for MG Midgets and Magnettes, the rolling chassis with engine, gearbox, radiator, and all running gear, quoted the following prices:

MG Midget PB–type   £175.0.0
MG Magnette N–type   £210.0.0

Several body builders worked closely with the Australian distributors of MG cars. Lanes Motors of Melbourne was the main importer and distributor of MG sports cars in the early 1930s and nearly all MGs prior to World War II, with the exception of TAs and TBs, came in without bodies. Lanes contracted a small but

innovative body builder, Chas Aspinal & Sons of High Street, Armadale, to do the work.

Racing drivers of the day preferred these Aspinal–bodied MGs. Being built on a narrow, rigid frame with high scuttles and deep cut–aways instead of doors, they were ideal for racing. Because they were all–metal and did not have door openings, they were more rigid, and were thus more durable than the wooden–framed English bodies.

The rough dirt race tracks of the day, such as Phillip Island, would shake the wooden–framed bodies to pieces.

The Aspinal–bodied J, P, F, L, and N–type MGs had a string of racing successes. Les Jennings (F and L–types), Les Murphy (P–type), Robert McKay (P–type) and Colin Keefer (J–type), all raced Aspinal bodied MGs.

These bodies finally went out of fashion in the 1950s as the lack of doors usually required the hood to be drawn back for the occupants to enter or exit the cockpit. Some MG owners subsequently fitted doors to the Aspinal bodies, or replaced them completely with English bodies, which were far more practical for everyday use. The Aspinal bodies, however, represent an important part of pre–war Australian MG history.

There were other companies in addition to Aspinal, of course, which made bodies for MGs

CHRONOLOGY

1931: 18/80 Mark I, MG 18/100 'Tigress' and MG Mark III discontinued. MG Magna F1, MG C–type racer and D–type saloon introduced. MG C–types are placed 1–2–3–4–5 in their first racing appearance at the Brooklands Double–12 race and become the first 750cc cars to lap the Brooklands outer circuit at over 100mph. Kimber employs John Thornley at MG Car Company.

1932: MG Magna F1, MG M–type Midget, D–type saloon and C–type racer discontinued. MG Magna F2 and F3, MG J1 and J2 sports cars and J3 and J4 racers introduced. Ron Horton drives an MG C–type to victory in the Brooklands 500 mile race. Cecil Kimber's ambition of two years previously had been achieved when, by Christmas 1932, MG held every International Class H record on the books.

1933: MG Magna F2 and F3, J1, J3, J4, 18/80 MK1 and Mk2 discontinued. MG Magnette K1, K2 and K3 and MG Magna L1 and L2 introduced. The K3 is widely regarded as the best racing car MG ever made and most successful 1100cc racing car ever made. It goes on to form the base for the record breaking EX135. George Eyston and Count Johnny Lurani drive a K3 to class and team wins in the Mille Miglia, its first race. Tazio Nuvolari drives the same car in Australia. A batch of 10 TA Midgets, for example, was shipped into Adelaide and Sydney in chassis form and fitted with Australian–made bodies which were almost identical to their English counterparts. And there are still in evidence today MG saloons with Australian–made bodies.

MGs NUMERICALLY DOMINANT ON THE CIRCUITS

The starting grid for the 1934 AGP clearly demonstrates the sudden popularity of the MG car in Australia — at least within the motor racing fraternity. Of the 21 cars entered, eight — more than a third of the field — were MGs: Thompson's 1087cc supercharged K3, Cec Warren in a 746cc supercharged J3 Midget, John Summers, Les Jennings and R Anderson in 1087cc unsupercharged L–type Magnas, Norman Putt in a K1 Magnette (listed as being 1286cc), plus Les Murphy and Jack Clements in 847cc MG J2 Midgets. MGs placed second, third, fourth and sixth, and the future of the marque on the racetracks and the roads of Australia was virtually sealed.

Thompson suffered a similar fate at the hands of the handicappers in the 1935 AGP at Phillip Island, once again setting fastest lap and fastest time, only to miss out by 31 seconds on catch-

CHRONOLOGY

to win the Ulster TT, breaking the Ards lap record seven times during the race. Eddie Hall drives an MG K3 to victory in the BRDC 500 mile race at Brooklands and James Wright drives an MG K3 prototype to break the 1100cc class record at the Mont des Mules hillclimb. Unfortunately, the MG K3 can only manage 64th out of 69 in the Monte Carlo Rally. Still the K3 becomes the first 1100cc car to exceed 120mph, 150mph and 200mph. Les Jennings places third in the Australian GP at Phillip Island with an F–type MG Magna. John Thornley is appointed as Service Manager at MG.

1934: Driven by George Eyston at Montlhéry in France, the MG EX135 with a 1087cc six–cylinder supercharged engine breaks the 1 km, 1 mile, 5 km, 5 miles, 10 km, 10 miles, 50 km, 50 miles, 100 km, 100 miles, 200 km and 1 hour Class G (up to 1100cc) speed records. MG J–types and MG Magnette K2 and K3 discontinued. MG PA sports car, MG Magnette NA and NE (only seven built) and MG QA racer (only eight built) introduced. William Morris elevated to the peerage. The Marshall Roots type supercharger replaces the Powerplus vane unit in the MG K3. George Eyston's MG K3 wins the British Empire Trophy at Brooklands. Eight MGs are entered for the Australian GP at Phillip Island, taking second, third, fourth and sixth places.

ing the winning MG P–type of Les Murphy.

Interestingly, Les Murphy's garage and car sales establishment at St Kilda Junction, Victoria was now a sub–agent for MGs to Lanes Motors. Robert M. Lane, son of the founder, Robert T. Lane, reports that his father died in 1943. Lane Jnr went on to manage the family business until 1984 when he sold out and retired, later to get itchy feet and to establish Lane Jaguar Rover. In the late 1980s Lane bought and restored an MG SA saloon similar to that which his father used as his private car in 1937.

Meanwhile, MGs continued to excel in Australia's premier motor race, the Australian Grand Prix. That 1935 event, the last at Phillip Island, was a rout of the opposition by the MG marque. Behind Les Murphy's P–type and Bill Thompson's K3 came Les Jennings' L–type Magna, and Bob McKay's P–type, while Tom Hollinrake drove the supercharged J3 which finished sixth. Eight of the 18 starters were in MGs.

At Victor Harbor in December 1936, Les Murphy's P–type won again from Tim Joshua's P–type, with John Summers' MG L–type Magna in eighth, and John Dutton's supercharged MG C–type 10th. Also in 1936, lady racer Joan Richmond from Melbourne, who had driven a Riley overland from Australia to England (via Darwin, Singapore, Penang, Calcutta, Bombay, Basra, Baghdad, Cairo, the Monte Carlo Rally — starting from Sicily, and Paris to London), drove an MG P–type for Captain George Eyston's team in the Le Mans 24 Hour Race, and finished. Miss Richmond had been the first lady to drive in the Australian Grand Prix, finishing 5th outright and second in class B in the 1931 AGP at Phillip Island in a 1087cc Riley.

In 1938 the GP (which was not run in 1937) moved to the new Mount Panorama circuit at Bathurst, then still an unsealed dirt road. The MGs were no match for Englishman Peter Whitehead's rapid ERA, but then nor was anything else in the race. John Sherwood in Alan Crago's T–type was third, the similar car of then–19–year–old John Crouch (who'd been the first to race a T–type in Australia when he ran this car at Penrith Speedway) was fifth, Les Murphy's P–type was ninth.

One of the greatest of all MG triumphs, however, was in the 1939 Australian Grand Prix when 22–years–old Perth racer Alan Tomlinson scored a well–paced victory on the high speed Lobethal road circuit in South Australia with a racing–bodied and immaculately prepared TA Special. Other MGs were well down the order, placing 9–10–11–12– and–15.

MG SALES NUMBERS PRIOR TO WW2

Though little has been recorded of sales numbers of MGs in the pre World War Two era, it has been stated by MG historians that most models of MG have come to Australia — if not when new, at least imported later when they became collector's items. Import records show that Lanes Motors received exactly 100 pre–war MGs. The shipments started late 1932 or early 1933. It should also be remembered that while Lanes in Victoria and Williams in NSW were official agents after about 1933, quite a few of the very desirable MGs were imported privately both before and after the appointment of these official agents.

These private imports were usually second–hand examples in either very good or even "as new" condition.

A story in an MG Car Club magazine 'Opposite Lock' suggests that of the rarer racing cars, six K3s came to Australia (only 33 were built), two Q–types (plus a replica built from a PA), and the 'Montlhéry' J3 record breaking car, which raced here before WW2. Australian MG enthusiast and owner, Pip Bucknell, tells us that the first 'pre–raced' MG K3 arrived here in 1934 on board the SS Port Huron.

The J3, two NE Magnettes, and at least some of the K3s came into Australia as private imports. We might never unearth the exact figures for total pre–war imports of MGs, but a very large percentage of them found their way onto the race circuits. Those imported purely for road use were relatively few in number.

As a young boy growing up in the 1950s, I remember that pre–T–type MGs were very scarce on the roads of Australia. To see one was to stop and watch it go by. My father recently confirmed this, and he was a keen fan of the marque. In 1951, as an eight year–old, I went with him as he shopped around the MG specialists of Sydney intending to buy an example of the marque. The bulk of the cars we saw were T–types, with just the occasional saloon model of the 1930s era and odd examples of rarer sports models.

CHRONOLOGY

1935: Lord Nuffield (William Morris) sells MG, Wolseley and other interests to Morris Motors Pty Ltd. Morris then becomes known as the Nuffield Organisation. MG withdraws from racing immediately. OHC engines are dropped from MG models built over the next four years and replaced by OHV pushrod engines. MG Magnette K1 and NA and MG Magna L1 and L2 discontinued. MG Magnette NB, MG PB sports car and MG R racer (only 10 built) introduced. MG R wins 750cc class in French Grand Prix. MG R is MG's only single seater racing car and the last racing Midget. The body is streamlined like the German Grand Prix cars of the day. The PB is last OHC Midget. Les Murphy leads home a 1–2–3–4–6 finish in the Australian GP at Phillip Island with his P–type.

1936: MG Magnette NB discontinued. MG PA and PB discontinued. MG SA/WA and MG TA introduced. Les Murphy wins the Australian GP again, this time at Victor Harbor in South Australia, with his P–type, followed home by another P–type in second place. MG takes World 750cc speed record at 140.6 mph.

1937: In February George Eyston puts his MG 'Magic Magnette' up for sale at Bellevue Garages, included were 'many spares, including track and road racing bodies' for £425. MG VA introduced.

CHRONOLOGY

1938: Morris takes over Riley. The 1087cc six–cylinder supercharged MG EX135 breaks the 1 km and 1 mile Class G (up to 1100cc) speed records at Frankfurt in Germany with Major Goldie Gardner at the wheel. Lord Nuffield becomes a Viscount. George Harriman is Works Superintendent. Syd Enever becomes MG's chief planning engineer.

1939: MG TB introduced (only 379 built). The 1 km, 1 mile and 5 km Class G (up to 1100cc) speed records are broken by the 1087cc six–cylinder supercharged MG EX135 driven by Major Goldie Gardner in Dessau in Germany. Two days later on July 6 the same car and driver break the 1 km, 1 mile and 5 km Class F (up to 1500cc) speed records with a 1500cc supercharged six–cylinder engine. Perth driver Alan Tomlinson (22) becomes the youngest ever winner of the Australian GP with his MG TA Special, at Lobethal in South Australia. Production halted at the outbreak of war. Factory given over for armaments production. MG SA, VA and TA discontinued. John Thornley called up for war service on outbreak of WW2.

1940: Leonard Lord and George Harriman move to the Morris company's rival Austin. MG TB released in Australia

My father finally settled on a 1935 NA Magnette, a fabulous looking four–seater that looked like a two–seater at first sight. It was cream, with red mudguards, and was registered in NSW with the number TM–011. It was virtually standard, apart from a copper tail–pipe for the exhaust system, which gave it a sensational exhaust note from its small 1271cc six–cylinder engine. It was quite claustrophobic sitting in the small rear seat with the hood up but, with the hood down, it was glorious. We drove from our home in Sutherland Shire to Mount Druitt to see a motor race meeting on the old airstrip there in 1951 and, of course, a very large percentage of the cars racing were MGs or MG Specials — as was to be the case for most of the 1950s.

One of the heroes of the 1940s–50s era in MGs was A.H. 'Curly' Brydon, who had a series of T–series based racers and had a service and repair garage near Kings Cross at that time, before becoming an executive on a Sydney newspaper. Brydon used to chew gum while he was driving and we kids, in the mid–50s, thought it would be 'cool' to chew the same brand. To this end we looked through the window of his road–car, an MG saloon, to see if we could see the gum packets. The only MG saloon we were familiar with at the time was the postwar Y–type, but this car was much larger. It was more than 30 years later, after his retirement from his management position with a New York (USA) newspaper, that I had dinner with Brydon and was finally able to ask if he remembered the car. He did, very well, and said it was a black SA saloon, which he enjoyed as his road car for quite some time.

Biggest sellers of the various MG models, in England, had been the 1928–1932 M–type Midget (3235 sold), the J1 and J2 (2463 sold), the PA and PB Midgets (2499 sold), and the SA saloon (2738 sold). The TA and TB models, built from 1936 to 1939, were to sell 3382 examples, and the VA saloon 2407, before WW2 interrupted. Of these, the T–series cars were the most numerous in Australia, and they were to completely transform the motor racing scene, bringing competitive machinery within the reach of more people than had ever before seemed possible. At the time of writing, the Pre–War MG Register of Australia included the following cars: One 14/28, three 14/40, three 18/80, twenty–three M–type, one C–type, forty–one J2, six J3, forty–five PA, eleven PB, two QA, one RA, sixty–two TA, twenty TB, ten F–type Magna, sixteen L–type Magna, four K1 Magnette, seven K3 Magnette, two KN, twelve NA, five NB, one ND, one NE, twenty–eight SA, six VA, and five WA, models.

TC A BIG SELLER IN AUSTRALIA

After the politicians, generals and Fuehrers had finished playing their silly war games of the 1940s, MG returned to the roads late in 1945 with the TC sports car, a development of the TA and TB. The TC was first sold in Australia early in 1946. Between 1945 and 1949 it was to sell 10,000 examples worldwide, an astronomical leap beyond any previous MG model's best sales effort.

In the late 1970s, Australian MG historian Rob Dunsterville wrote a letter to an enthusiast magazine I published and edited at the time, Cars and Drivers Australia. Dunsterville quoted some figures he had unearthed from records kept by P. & R. Williams, the NSW distributors for MG cars. These showed that 40 TCs were sold in 1946 (the model's first year in this country), 60–odd in 1947, more than 100 in 1948, almost 350 in 1949, and just under 100 in 1950. This was for NSW only, sold by Williams and other MG dealers such as the long–standing Parramatta Road MG dealer Ron Ward. Of the 10,000 TCs built, 2000 were exported to the USA. With 650 sold in NSW, it is reasonable to assume, given the enthusiasm for the marque in Victoria, that Australia accounted for more than 1000 TCs. The USA, in terms of sales, was to even more enthusiasti–cally embrace the MG TD which replaced the TC, taking a staggering 20,000 of the total 30,000 production run.

The TC was in fact a car well behind the trends of the time. It was a design that had been quite basic — as the original T–type — in the mid–1930s, yet the TC was still selling strongly 15 years later. Perhaps it was nostalgia, a yearning for the simplicity of life as it had been before the war, but it was also that the TC was an affordable fun car and people were keen to have fun in the late 1940s and early 1950s, to shake off the memories of a world at war.

TCs became more and more common on the roads and on the racetracks of Australia. It wasn't long before MGs in general, and TCs in particular, were to dominate the entry lists of many motoring competitions, from reliability trials to mud–trials, hill climbs, and circuit racing. They were even to carry on the tradition established in the 1930s of winning an occasional Australian Grand Prix, and certainly gaining many of the major placings. In its June 1946 issue, that great magazine of the 1940s and 1950s, Australian Motor Sports (AMS), carried a two page test/review of the 1946 MG TC. The story begins: 'Just released by the Australian agents is the new version of the popular MG Midget series, known as the TC. This model is similar to the TB that was produced just prior to the war. There were a few of these models sold in this country before the commencement of hostilities. The new TC is an open two–seater of typical Midget style — the established price is understood to be 594 pounds 10 shillings plus sales tax (Melbourne)'.

John Crouch, the first man to race a T–type in Australia, back in 1938, now became the first man to race a TC in Australia in 1946, gaining two second places at the Strathpine meeting in Queensland. Shortly afterwards, at Bathurst, the Under–1500cc Handicap had 15 entries, nine of which were MGs (three TAs, three TBs, one TC for A.V. 'Alby' Johnson, one NE, and one P–type). In the NSW Grand Prix over 100 miles at Bathurst Alf Najar's MG TB Special was first home, ahead of John

Nind's TA and Johnson's TC in second and third. Motor racing in 1947 continued to feature MGs. In the Victoria Cup at Ballarat, MG TCs were third and fourth (Eadie and Nind), with an MG P–type 12th (J. Hoy). In NSW, MG TAs, TBs, TCs, an NE Magnette, a J2, and an L–type Magna dominated the results of the supporting races at Marsden Park Airstrip.

Lanes Motors was still selling MGs in style, as evidenced by a full page advertisement in the July 1947 AMS for: 'Lanes Motors Pty Ltd 89–109 Exhibition Street Melbourne. Sole distributors in Victoria and Southern Riverina of MG TC Sports Roadsters and Series Y Saloons'. The ad pointed out that MG was 'Winner of the 1st, 2nd, and 3rd places in the Championship of NSW, and 1st, 2nd and 3rd in the under 1500cc Championship at King's Birthday Races on the famous Nowra circuit'. Adding: 'Details of the new MG Series Y English body saloons will be announced at a later date'.

MG WINS AUSTRALIAN GP — AGAIN

The Australian GP returned to Bathurst in 1947, the first postwar running of the event. Twelve of the 28 entries were MGs, and the race was won on handicap by Bill Murray in a stripped MG TC. Other MGs finished in positions 6–8–9–10–11–13–14. And so it continued in 1948: Thirteen of the 51 nominations (25 per cent) for the Australian GP at Point Cook (only 25 to be accepted) were MGs. These were made up of five TCs, two TAs, two TBs, and one each of the K3, NE, PA, and QA models.

With all this promotion of the MG marque on the race circuits, the TC was selling gangbusters in the showrooms, rolling out the doors faster than any sports car had ever done before in this country. Supply was erratic, however, and there were often long 'droughts' of MG models until new shipments became available from the UK. Late in 1947 the TC had been joined in Australia by the desirable little MG Y saloon, which shared the engine (though only in single carburettor form) and other components with the TC. The January edition of AMS carried a roadtest of this car, headed: 'The New MG Model 1¼ Litre — A Family Sports Car'. No retail price was mentioned.

Supply problems with the MG TC and Y were alleviated late in 1948, as evidenced by a full–page ad in both the September and October issues of AMS for Lanes Motors Pty Ltd. The company proudly announced that: 'Shipments have now arrived from England and prompt delivery is assured'.

The car had already been on sale in this country for three years when, in the January 1949 issue, Australian Motor Sports magazine decided it was time to run another roadtest of an MG TC. There was no story, however; the article was in the form of tables of specifications and test results figures, with just one press hand–out picture. The price of the TC was listed at £641, plus tax. Acceleration times included: 19.5 seconds for 0–60mph, and 21.5 seconds for the standing–start ¼–mile. A top speed of 77.6mph was attained, at which point the speedometer was reading 83mph. Overall fuel consumption, including the performance testing was 31mpg. AMS noted that the car was 'Fully described in AMS for June 1946'.

MGs were prominent once again in the Australian GP of 1949, run this time at Leyburn in Queensland. Behind ex–MG racer John Crouch's magnificent 3.6–litre Delahaye, which won, was Ray 'Laddie' Gordon's MG TC in second, Peter Critchley's MG TB Special in fourth, 'Curly' Brydon's MG TC in sixth, and two more TCs ninth and tenth.

Jack Old's Monaro Motors in Malvern Victoria, was at this time advertising various components for MGs. For example: '...cast aluminium cooling fins for T–type MG brake drums; instrument panel grab handles embossed with MG emblem, designed by us to match the rest of the fittings on T–types; cast aluminium rocker covers with large bronze cap embossed with MG emblem; Arnott superchargers complete with all fittings and special carburettors for MG series TC'. The ad concluded: 'We specialise in the servicing and repair and tuning of all the MG models from 1938 on..'.

Eighteen of the 42 cars entered for the 1950 Australian GP at Nuriootpa, South Australia, in January, were MGs: 10 TC or TC Specials, three K3 Magnettes, two N–type Magnettes, one P–type, and one TB, plus an MG–Vauxhall. In NSW Nat Buchanan had begun competing in his Y–type saloon. From the mid–

1950s Buchanan was to become well–known throughout Australia for the design and building of Buchanan fibreglass bodies. Moulded from Tom Sulman's 1955 Aston Martin DB3S, these were fitted to numerous chassis. A common formula for a Buchanan–bodied special was the MG TC chassis, with either the MG or a Holden engine fitted.

THE TD IS A BIG SELLER WORLDWIDE

MG drivers and followers had taken to the TC like no other MG before it, but its days in the new car showrooms were over. The MG TD was introduced to Australia early in 1950 and, in the April 1950 edition of AMS, there was a roadtest and story on 'The MG Midget Series TD' with the sub–heading: 'Chassis Redesigned, IFS, Rack and Pinion Steering'. The story carries a number of interesting observations: 'The most apparent outward change is the substitution of bolt–on pressed steel disc wheels for the centre–lock wire wheels, the manufacturers giving as their reason for this substitution that it is necessary because of design considerations to do with the independent front suspension'. The story continues: 'Though earlier rumours had it that the TD would use a modified and tuned version of the overhead camshaft 4/50 Wolseley unit, on the face of it a most suitable power unit, the well known and well tried four–cylinder pushrod engine common to the Series TB and TC cars is retained'; 'Electrically welded throughout, the chassis frame is a completely new design'; 'Brakes, although they have the same drum diameter as those of the TC, now have two leading shoes in the front...'; and, amusingly, 'By using hypoid bevel final drive, it has been possible to dispense with a good deal of the central hump of the TC, so that three passengers can be accommodated abreast with considerably less discomfort than before'. All of them very good friends, we hope...

In the excellent book 'MG by McComb' the author, F. Wilson McComb, says of the TD: 'So the TC owners were as loud in their disdain for the TD as, fourteen years earlier, the PB owners had been in their scorn for the TA. In terms of sales, however, the TD proceeded to knock the TC into a cocked hat, and exports soared almost out of sight'.

In 1951 the TD lost its original slotted steel wheels and was fitted with better–looking drilled steel wheels. Late in 1952, the TD Mark II was introduced in England with larger twin SU carburettors which helped to raise the power output from the original 54.4bhp (40.6kW) at 5200rpm to a claimed 57bhp (42.5kW) at 5500rpm. However, the seemingly insatiable appetite of American sports car lovers for the TD meant that MG was flat out supplying that market and had few left over to send to Australia. Shipments to Australian distributors were inconsistent, to say the least.

The shortage of new MG TDs in the Australian dealerships was at an embarrassing level by early 1952, prompting B.S. Stillwell and Co — now an MG dealer — to run a full page ad in AMS March 1952 issue asking: 'MG Owners! No New TDs?... Then let us keep your present vehicle in first class order...'

At last, a few TDs trickled into the country in August 1952. An advertisement from Lanes Motors Pty Ltd stated: 'Special Release! A limited number only of the famous MG TD model Sports Roadsters... Despite prior advice that no MG TD models would be available in Victoria, a special release of a small number has now been arranged. It is unlikely that further releases will be available. If you are a prospective TD buyer, phone, write or call without delay — this is your opportunity! A limited number only for immediate delivery'. Monaro Motors had a less dramatic ad, also full page but with the new Morris Minor convertible sharing the space with the TD: 'MG TDs — MG TDs — MG TDs now available, immediate delivery, price £1035... confidential terms available, 1240 Malvern Road, Malvern, Victoria'. B.S. Stillwell and Co advertised in the classified columns: 'MG TD — New iridescent grey–bronze with red leather trim. This car is at present in stock and is available for immediate delivery. £1035.'.

While various MGs and MG Specials continued to do well in lesser events, it seemed their days were numbered in major races like the Australian Grand Prix. The 1952 AGP at Bathurst in April saw the most successful MGs finish 8th, 9th, 12th and 13th. However, at the next AGP almost 19 months later, at Melbourne's Albert Park in November 1953, most of the front–running big cars dropped out and Doug Whiteford's winning 4.5–litre GP Lago–Talbot was followed home by Curly Brydon's MG Special in second, the now–20–years–old MG K3 of Andy Brown in third, and the also–venerable MG Q–type of Les Murphy in fourth place. As well, the AGP, in 1949 and since 1951, had been run as a scratch event, so the MGs had finished on their merit, not by virtue of an easy handicap.

THE LAST TRADITIONAL MG SQUARE RIGGER

In 1954 Australia got a new motoring magazine and a new MG sports car; a bright

---

CHRONOLOGY

1948: Using a Jaguar XJ–type 1999cc four–cylinder twin OHC engined EX135, Major Goldie Gardner sets new 1 km, 1 mile and 5 km Class E (up to 2000cc) speed records. Alf Najar's MG TB Special finishes second in the Australian GP at Point Cook.

1949: Production of Riley cars moves from Coventry to Abingdon. MG TC imports discontinued in Australia. MG TD introduced in GB. Major Goldie Gardner sets new Class I (up to 500cc) speed records in EX135 with a supercharged MG 995cc six–cylinder engine running on only three cylinders to make 497cc at Jabbeke in Belgium. John Thornley appointed assistant general manager of MG. Ray Gordon in an MG TC finishes second in the Australian GP at Leyburn in Queensland.

1950: MG TD released in Australia. MG TD MkII replaces MkI in GB. Running on only two of its six cylinders (making 332cc) a 995cc six–cylinder supercharged engine powers Major Goldie Gardner and the EX135

CHRONOLOGY

to new Class J (up to 350cc) speed records at Jabbeke in Belgium. MG Specials finish fourth, sixth, seventh, eighth, twelfth and thirteenth on actual time in the Australian GP at Nuriootpa, SA.

1951: New 50 km, 50 mile, 100 km, 100 mile, 200 km and 1 hour Class F (up to 1500cc) speed records are set by Major Goldie Gardner at Utah, USA in the MG XPAG 1250cc four–cylinder supercharged EX135. A special bodied MG TD is built for George Phillips to race at Le Mans and forms the basis for EX175, the MGA prototype. MG TCs finish 3–5–6–7 in Australian GP at Narrogin in Western Australia.

1952: Nuffield and Austin merged to form BMC. Lord Nuffield steps down from the chairmanship of the Nuffield Organisation and becomes the corporation's honorary president. Former Morris employee, Austin chairman and architect of the Austin/Morris merger, Leonard Lord becomes first chairman of BMC. Powered by a VC–20–G 1973cc six–cylinder supercharged engine EX135 breaks the 50 km, 50 miles and 100 km Class E (up to 2000cc)

red MG TF adorned the cover of the very first issue of Modern MOTOR magazine, dated June 1954. Unfortunately there was no road test of the car in that issue, merely a five–page story on MGs in general, with very little Australian content. But it did demonstrate the magazine's publishers' respect for the MG marque that they selected the TF for that all–important first cover. The 'What They Cost' pages showed the MG TF was listed at a very reasonable £982, when three Holden models ranged from £1023 to £1075, the Austin–Healey 100 was £1391, and the Jaguar XK120 ranged from £1950 to £2150.

The MG TF road test came in the July issue of Modern MOTOR, in which Barrie Louden under the heading 'Performer Plus' wrote: 'Streamlining and certain alterations to body shape have not changed the traditional MG character'. He summed up the car: 'In all I found the MG a sheer delight to drive. It handles perfectly, offers a lively performance, and inspires confidence and safety...'

Power for the MG TF was the same 1250cc engine producing a claimed 57bhp (42.5kW) that had been fitted to the TD Mark II. In England the TF was fitted with bolt–on drilled steel wheels, similar to those on the TD. Wire–spoke wheels were an extra–cost option. In Australia, however, TFs were sold only with the wire wheels. In later years there was the occasional private import of a second hand TF with steel wheels, but these were a rarity. There was actually very little that was different about

the TF, compared to the TD Mark II, and yet it was a very clever update, because the car looked much more modern, and certainly much prettier. The bonnet line now sloped downwards from the windscreen forwards, a lower radiator grille sloped rearwards and had a curved line to it, the headlights were faired into the front mudguards, and the rear of the car was sloped forwards — nicely complementing the rakish front.

Inside the TF, the single–piece seat squab of the TD, with separate base for each passenger, now gave way to two separate bucket seats which located the occupants much better than the older design seats did.

Although the TF was well received by the motoring press in Australia, MG historian McComb writes that 'British pressmen merely damned it with faint praise...' In the US, the car was described as 'a big disappointment.' The reason for this was that MG enthusiasts had been teased by reports of a much more modern full–width aerodynamic design for the past three years. MG had entered such a car in the Le Mans 24 Hour Race of 1951 and the EX175 second prototype was wind tunnel tested as a potential speed record breaking car in 1953 and 1954. It was to eventually (in 1955) become the MGA.

Jaguar had released the sensational–looking XK120 years earlier and now Austin had the beautiful Austin Healey 100 — released while MG was still selling the TD in ever decreasing numbers. The MG TF — like the TD — was also an inexpensive car, but there was no escaping the fact that, as pretty as it was, it was now an outdated design. First Australian competition appearance for the MG TF was in 1954.

At the time of writing, the Australian MGT Register shows the following T–type MG population in Australia: fifty–six TA, twenty–one TB, 568 TC, 530 TD, 341 TF, 114 Y–type, and 186 Z Magnettes.

A MODERN SALOON CAR JOINS THE RANKS

In September 1954 the first Sydney Motor Show was announced and so, too, was the MG Magnette saloon, which BMC rushed to Australia to star in that show. Modern MOTOR

CHRONOLOGY

speed records at Utah, USA with Major Goldie Gardner driving. Two days later Gardner drives the EX135 this time with an MG XPAG 1250cc four–cylinder supercharged engine to the Class F (up to 1500cc) 5 mile and 10 km speed records. EX175, the MGA prototype designed by Syd Enever, is built but permission to proceed is turned down by BMC management. John Thornley promoted to General Manager of MG. Nuccio Bertone commissions Franco Scaglione to design a GT coupe body for an MG TD running chassis which subsequently becomes known as the 'Arnolt–MG' after Chicago based importer 'Wacky' Arnolt orders 200. MG TD MkII replaces MkI in Australia.

1953: MG Y and MG TD MkII discontinued in GB and Australia. MG TD MkIIA introduced in GB (47 competition cars built). MG TF (1250cc) introduced in GB and Australia. MG Magnette ZA introduced in GB to become the first MG with a unitary body construction and the first to be fitted with the B–series engine. MGs finish second, third and fourth in Australian GP at Albert Park, Melbourne.

pointed out that the Magnette ZA was '... the first MG to have a mono–construction body and chassis...' and, '... apart from the traditional (though curved) MG radiator, the body is like that of the current Wolseley 4/44 — but in everything else, it's a vastly different car...' Modern MOTOR also added that all of the first small shipment of cars, due in September, were 'covered by orders'. The same issue carried a full–page, all–colour advertisement for the Magnette.

The engine in the ZA Magnette was different from the XPAG engine in the TF, being a push–rod OHV four–cylinder with bore and stroke of 73mm x 88.9mm to give a capacity of 1489cc and a power output of 60bhp (44.8kW) at 4600rpm.

In 1955 the MG TF was updated mechanically by the fitting of the larger 72mm x 90mm, 1466cc XPEG '1500' engine, which produced a claimed 63bhp (47kW) at 5000rpm. It was a far more flexible, as well as more powerful, engine. The TF had '1500' badges added to the sides of the bonnet and two red reflectors on the rear of the body to distinguish it from the earlier 1250.

The TF 1500 went on sale in Australia in June 1955, with the price unchanged from the 1250cc version, at £982. In September, Modern MOTOR ran a story on: 'MG Production Racer — Le Mans was a try–out for prototype of future models', showing a photo and drawings of the Le Mans car, looking very much like what would later become the long–awaited MGA. Modern MOTOR said of the MG people: '...They added that if the car continued to please them, the next MG production models would have a lot in common with the prototypes. And they would sell at a very competitive price'.

'New Cars for 56' was the cover story in December 1955, with the MGA, bright red of course, sharing the cover with a 2.4–litre Jaguar saloon. 'You'll like the new MG' predicted Harold Dvoretsky in his three–page story within. 'The only resemblance between the new MGA Series model and its predecessors is a faint likeness in the radiator grille...' The engine was based on the BMC 'B' Series as used in the MG Magnette ZA, still 1489cc, but was more highly developed to produce

68bhp (50.7kW) at 5500rpm. Weight of the MGA was down from the TF's 17.75cwt (902.6kg) to 17.0cwt (864.4kg). Dvoretsky predicted the MGA would be on display in Australia around Christmas time 1955 but deliveries would not take place until April or May 1956. In March 1956, however, the price of the MGA was listed in 'What They Cost' as £1147.

As with the TF, in England the MGA came standard with steel wheels, with wire wheels as an option; in Australia, wire wheels were standard.

It wasn't until the July 1956 issue that Modern MOTOR was able to roadtest the MGA. List price of the MGA was now noted as £1256, while the Triumph TR3A tested in the same issue was £1630, so the pricing was certainly competitive.

Bryan Hanrahan, who tested the MGA, declared it 'as good as it looks'. Hanrahan noted that half the production run of MGAs was shipped straight to America and '... that means we don't get many at all...' He goes on to point out: '... Don't compare the car's performance with either the Triumph or the Austin–Healey... Engine capacity is half–a–litre down on the Triumph and a full litre less than the Austin–Healey...'

Summing up the MGA, Hanrahan wrote: '...the A is a grand machine, in the best MG tradition. First of a New Line the manufacturers say. Let's hope it's a long one; and that import restrictions and a fine British product do not, paradoxically, continue for long to make

CHRONOLOGY

1954: MG TF (1250cc) is replaced by MG TF 1500 in GB. BMC allows the re–opening of the drawing office at MG. Syd Enever becomes chief engineer at MG and gives the go–ahead to produce the MGA which becomes the first postwar model officially designed on the premises. BMC chairman Leonard Lord knighted. 'Curly' Brydon finishes second for the second successive year with an MG Special in the Australian GP, this time at Southport, Qld.

1955: MG TF 1500 introduced in Australia. MG TF 1500 discontinued in GB and replaced by MGA.

1956: George Harriman appointed Deputy Chairman of BMC. John Thornley appointed Director of MG Car Company. MGA introduced in Australia with 1489cc four–cylinder B series (tuned version of Magnette saloon) engine. The MGA is the first all new MG since before WW2 and the first MG with all–enveloping bodywork. The Australian GP, for the first time since 1933, does not have an MG on the starting grid.

one wish he was in America'.

A fixed–top coupe version of the MGA, fully lockable and with wind–up windows, appeared in the Australian price lists late in 1958, though a price wasn't shown until January 1959, when it was listed at £1778 compared with the open version at £1376.

A BRAVE, BUT LESS THAN SUCCESSFUL, EFFORT

In July 1958, BMC released the MGA Twin Cam, a version of the car aimed primarily at motor sport. It had, as the name implies, a twin–overhead camshaft head, higher compression ratio, a stronger bottom end, and a larger bore diameter of 75.4mm to raise capacity to 1588cc — just under the racing 1600cc class limit. It was also fitted with disc brakes on all four wheels. But the Twin Cam was too late to be really successful on the circuits; it was the era of purpose–built sports–racing cars and the MG was out–gunned. As well, the Twin Cam, which developed 108bhp (80.6kW) at a very high 6700rpm compared with the later MGA 1500's 72bhp (53.7kW) at 5500rpm, proved to be unreliable. Modern MOTOR roadtested a Twin Cam in the August 1959 issue and the price was quoted at £1867. Only a few came to Australia and most of them were used in competition at one time or another. Robin Orlando's was the most successful, but Twin Cams generally were plagued with minor problems including chronic oil leaks. In the

US, which was MG's major market, many owners were over–revving the engines and blowing them asunder; the Twin Cam's mechanical woes were giving the marque a bad name and production ceased early in 1960 after only 2111 had been built.

Something less than a big seller on the Australian market was the MG Magnette Mark III, introduced in 1959. This was another of BMC's 'badge–engineering' exercises, the car being based on the Austin A55/Morris Oxford with Farina styling. But, at 66.5bhp (49.6kW), the MG version had more power than its close kin, the gear ratios were of a more sporting nature, and it had 14–inch wheels in place of their 15–inch units, a fact which road tester Bryan Hanrahan claimed transformed the MG's handling. It was priced at £1722 and was never more than a rarity on Aussie roads. Its replacement with the Mark IV in 1961 went virtually unnoticed and the Magnette disappeared from the Australian sales price lists in 1964, despite remaining in production in the UK until 1968.

Meanwhile, in October 1960, BMC in Australia had rolled the first locally–assembled MGA off its production line at Zetland, in Sydney. BMC had been assembling family cars on this line for some years by that time and the production rate of the MGA was up to three cars a day by 1961, far exceeding the small run of Triumph TR3s coming out of the Standard factory in Melbourne.

Big news of 1961 in England was the return of the MG Midget, the name used for the most popular small MG sports cars of the 1930s, 40s, and 50s, culminating with the TF in the mid–50s, but absent from the model line–up since then. This was, in fact, a development of the old 'bug-eye' Austin Healey Sprite and, in typical BMC style there was, of course, an Austin Healey Sprite version which was little different from the Midget. When the model did come to Australia, it was as the Austin Healey Sprite Mark II, the MG Midget being strangely absent from the Aussie sales lists.

Beating that car to Australia by a small margin — in April 1962 — was the MGA Mark II, with subtle and not necessarily attractive changes to the grille and other minor body fitments plus, more importantly, a more robust engine. Capacity had gone up to 1622cc

CHRONOLOGY

1957: Production of Austin–Healeys moves to Abingdon. Stirling Moss drives the MG EX181 to set a Class E (up to 1500cc) speed record of 245.6mph (395.4km/h) on the Utah salt flats.

1958: MG Magnette ZA/ZB discontinued. MGA Twin Cam introduced. Don Hayter completes first pencil drawing of MGB, code–named EX214/1. Later in the year he takes over MG's Project's Department.

1959: Phil Hill drives the MG EX181 to a Class F (up to 2000cc) speed record of 254.9mph (410.4km/h) on the Utah salt flats. This was MG's last record attempt.

1960: MGA Twin Cam discontinued. MG assembles small number of Morris Minor traveller and van models for next four years. Assembly of MGA 1600 MkIs begins in Australia. Four MG Specials take the starting grid for the Australian GP at Lowood in Queensland — the last time the marque is raced in Australia's major racing car event.

by increasing the bore to 76.2mm; power was up to 93bhp (69.4kW) at 5500rpm in the UK, though in Australia a lower 8.3:1 compression ratio dropped this to 90bhp (67.1kW). The potential for increased acceleration was diminished by the fitting of a 4.1:1 final drive ratio in place of the former 4.3:1, but at least this improved the top speed and reduced mechanical noise at normal touring speeds. Introductory price in Australia remained at the £1313 of the superseded model.

IN THE MG ALPHABET, B IS FOR BIG–SELLER

Production sports car racing introduced in the early 1960s, principally at Warwick Farm, gave MG a brief comeback in motor sport in this country, with a few MGAs being competitive on the circuits. The MGA's replacement, the MG MGB (MG was the maker's name, MGA and MGB were, rather confusingly, the model names), which arrived in Australia in May 1963 and sold for £1365, had an even larger engine — now 1798cc — but it was a heavier car than the MGA, at 18.5cwt (940.7kg). The MGB used mono–construction, without a separate chassis and looked more modern than the MGA, although not as pretty.

Power output for the MGB was claimed at 95bhp (70.8kW) at 5400rpm. The old B–Series BMC engine retained its original 89.0mm

CHRONOLOGY

1961: MGA 1600 MkII replaces MkI in the UK. MG Midget released in Australia. Initially available with 948cc A series four–cylinder engine (then later with 1098cc four–cylinder engine), it is the first MG since 1936 to have an engine of less than 1 litre. Sir Leonard Lord hands over chairmanship of BMC to George Harriman.

1962: MGB released at the Earls Court Motor Show. MGA 1600 MkII introduced in Australia. MGA discontinued in GB and Australia. MG 1100/1300 saloons introduced in GB. Sir Leonard Lord becomes Lord Lambury.

1963: Assembly of MGBs in Australia begins. 444 MGBs sold in Australia. William Morris (Lord Nuffield) dies. The MGB makes its racing debut in the Sebring 12 Hour race. An MGB scores 12th outright and first in class at the Le Mans 24–Hour race. The Laycock overdrive is offered as an option on the MGB from the beginning of 1963.

stroke but the bore had now grown to almost 80.3mm. The MGB had disc brakes at the front, but retained drum units at the rear.

Some of the extra weight in this new car was a result of larger doors and wind–up glass windows in place of the former car's side–curtains. The MGB retained the traditional MG wire–spoked wheels, which are also weighty, apart from being less rigid than steel wheels — but that's what MG buyers expected. Saleswise, the MGB was enormously successful; the Mark I alone sold almost 138,000 cars between 1962 and 1967 — mostly in the US of course.

An even bigger seller, worldwide, was the MG 1100, based on the prosaic Morris 1100 but with 25 per cent more power, although this was never sold new in Australia (private imports in later years have seen MG 1100 numbers reach 30 in Australia at the time of writing). When the MGB Mark II replaced the original MGB in 1967 (1968 in Australia), it went on to sell 375,000 worldwide in its various forms, making more than half a million MGBs produced and sold all together. It was the biggest selling MG of all time.

From March 1965, in Australia, the MGB was delivered with a five–bearing block and crankshaft in place of the former three–bearing set–up, adding further strength to the unit.

As with the MGA before it, the MGB was assembled in Australia by BMC at its Zetland (Sydney) plant. Local content was progressively increased to a final 45 per cent before the car went out of production in 1972.

In the meantime, BMC finally brought the MG Midget to Australia in 1968. In a way, it had been here since 1961 — in the guise of the Austin–Healey Sprite Mark II and IIA. Now, the Sprite was discontinued and replaced by the MG Midget — purely a marketing exercise. The Midget was the Mark III version, with 1275cc engine similar to that in the Morris Cooper S. It produced 65bhp (48.5kW) at 6000rpm and provided a claimed top speed of 93.5mph (150.5km/h).

Modern MOTOR's testers were a little disappointed with the Midget at first acquaintance but, after driving it for a week, they were won over. 'We like it — despite our earlier misgivings', they said, 'We're sure young sports car enthusiasts will like it too'.

The Mark II version of the MGB was released in the UK late in 1967 but Australians had to wait until early 1969 to see the car. Modern MOTOR, in its March 1969 issue, declared the many subtle changes to be 'notable improvements', adding that the new car was '... quieter, more rigid, more weatherproof, more responsive, more roadworthy... safer, and more fun'.

Changes listed by BMC Australia (the title being still used, despite a merger between BMC and Leyland in England during 1968) included: automatic transmission as an option for the first time, revised gear ratios, synchromesh now also on first gear, improved gear shift linkage, new electric overdrive on third and fourth gears, antiburst door locks, recessed interior door handles, soft plastic window winders, new ventilation–demisting system, and a high output alternator. Confusing for future researchers of the marque were changes made to the Mark I in its last weeks and carried over to this new model, namely: radial–ply tyres, stronger front antiroll bar, oil cooler, reversing lights, laminated windscreen and headlamp flasher.

Also assembled in Australia, at BMC's Zetland plant, the new MGB and the locally–assembled Midget were claimed to be the only sports cars in the world to be Roto–dipped and rustproofed. In April 1970 the Midget scored an upgrade as well. BMC Australia had now become British Leyland Australia. The company claimed the leather–bound alloy steering wheel, multi–lace wire wheels, reclining seats, laminated windscreen and radial–ply tyres — all standard equipment, as well as oil cooler and antiroll bar — were extra–cost options in other countries. Seats were improved, as was the hood folding system, and matt–black mesh grille and lower sills, plus a new range of colours, had been included. A detachable hardtop and a press–button radio were extra cost options.

Hard on the updated Midget's heels came a revision of the MGB, which became known as the MGBL (for British Leyland) in Australia. It wasn't as new as the company tried to pretend, but it was distinguished by a matt–black grille with chrome strip insert, new front and rear badges and bonnet moulding, scuff plates on the sills, British Leyland symbol on the front guards, reclining seats with provision for head–restraints, and leather–bound alloy steering wheel. As with the Midget, the hood–folding mechanism had been redesigned, and a laminated windscreen and other refinements had been added. Factory kits were now available to improve performance through several stages to full racing tune.

But the MG's days were numbered in Australia. Government regulations were brought in that required locally assembled cars to have 85

CHRONOLOGY

1964: Paddy Hopkirk partners Andrew Hedges in an MGB in the 1964 Le Mans 24 Hour. They average 99.9mph (160.8km/h). 802 MGBs sold in Australia in 1964.

1965: BMC takes over Pressed Steel. BMC chairman George Harriman knighted. 915 MGBs sold in Australia in 1965. MGB GT introduced and described by MG general manager John Thornley as 'poor man's Aston Martin'. The new fixed roof is designed by Pininfarina.

1966: 1084 MGBs sold in Australia in 1966

1967: Lord Lambury (Leonard Lord) dies. MGC introduced. 1228 MGBs sold in Australia. BMC merges with Jaguar to form British Motor Holdings (BMH).

1968: BMC, BMH and Leyland merge to form British Leyland Motor Corporation (BLMC or BL). Sir George Harriman briefly becomes BL's first chairman before handing over to Donald Stokes. MG becomes part of the specialist car division with Jaguar, Daimler, Rover and Triumph. EX234 proposed as replacement for Midget and MGB. 1026 MGBs sold in Australia as MkI gives way to the

CHRONOLOGY

MkII. Overdrive becomes available with the MGB. An MGB GT and an MGB are entered in the 1968 Nurburgring Marathon; they are the last official Abingdon MG competition entries in a motor race. The Midget begins production in Australia with the 1275cc four–cylinder engine.

1969: MGC discontinued. Donald Stokes awarded life peerage. John Thornley retires from MG due to ill health. 1089 MGBs sold in Australia.

1970: 1053 MGBs sold in Australia as the MkII is replaced by the MGBL. The MGBL has the three–speed Borg–Warner 35 automatic transmission as an option and features a new folding hood mechanism designed by Italian stylist Michelotti.

1971: MG 1100/1300 saloons discontinued. 883 MGBs sold in Australia.

1972: Production of MGBs in Australia ends. Midget is also discontinued here. Regulations enforcing 85 percent local content in locally manufactured cars make production of low volume MGB uneconomical (Australian MGBs have 45 percent local content).

per cent Aussie content. This was impracticable for a low–volume car like the MGB and, in November 1972, Leyland Australia (the company name was changed so often in this era that few could ever remember what it was called 'this week') announced that production of the MGB in Australia would cease. Even worse for MG fans, there would be no imported cars bearing the octagon badge. The MGA had been assembled in Australia between 1960 and 1962, followed by a 10–year production run of the MGB from 1963 to 1972. Sales numbers of the MGB in Australia were quoted as: 1963 — 444; 1964 — 802; 1965 — 915; 1966 — 1084; 1967 — 1228; 1968 — 1026; 1969 — 1089; 1970 — 1053; 1971 — 883, for a total of 8524 (Leyland Australia somehow added this to a total of 'more than 9000').

And that was it for MG in Australia — for a couple of decades, anyway. The last time an MG appeared in the price lists in Modern MOTOR magazine was May 1973. Then, suddenly, it was gone. Enthusiasts continued to import cars privately in small numbers. The six–cylinder MGC, built in the UK between 1967 and 1969 had found the odd Aussie owner. Also popular was the MGB GT V8, a hard–top MGB with Rover 3500 V8 alloy engine built from late 1972 until mid–1976 in the UK. A few Australians imported these in the 1970s, but numbers accelerated rapidly in Australia in the early 1990s, with Australian entrepreneurs finding these models selling at very low prices overseas at that time. According to an MG Car Club source, numbers of the

CHRONOLOGY

1973: Don Hayter is appointed MG's chief engineer the last to hold the position. President and former chairman of British Leyland and BMC, Sir George Harriman, dies. MGB GT V8 introduced.

1974: The Midget gets the 1493cc four–cylinder Triumph engine in GB.

1975: BL announces that USA specification MGBs are to be sold in the UK.

1979: MG Midget discontinued in November.

1980: MGB discontinued in October. Abingdon factory closed down. Rumours that Aston–Martin would buy MG come to nothing.

1981: BL sell Abingdon factory to an insurance company for development as an industrial estate. A grand total of 1.1 million MGs has been produced of which 920,000 were sports cars. 970,000 were built at Abingdon along with 220,000 cars of other makes. Abingdon was the largest single sports car factory in the world and MG the most popular sports car make. Henry Ford II buys the last US spec MGB.

1992: Production of MG sports cars recommences with limited edition MG RV8, a V8–powered restyled version of the MGB.

MGC jumped from 30 in Australia to 60 or 70 in a couple of years. Similarly, local ownership of the MGB GT V8 leaped from about 30 to more than 50 in the same period. Even the 1493cc MG Midget built in the UK between late 1974 and late 1979, fitted with the US–style 'rubber nose' was snapped up from the US by a few Aussies. But there was little interest in things like MG Metro, Metro Turbo, Maestro and Montego — those badge–engineered saloons that carried the MG name through the 1980s in Britain.

In Australia, MG as a new car was absent for two decades — 1972 to 1992. Then, early in 1993, moves were made to officially import limited numbers of the MG RV8, an MGB convertible–based model with styling changes and a Rover V8 engine. As we went to press, however, these were said to be on hold. Despite the unexpected resurrection of MG sports cars, MG seems unlikely to regain its position as one of the most revered sports cars the world has ever seen. The glory days of MG will live on, however, in the memories of many enthusiasts, as well as being the subject of motoring history books. And MG cars of all ages will be seen at vintage car meetings for as long as such events exist.

LINEUP OF MAJOR MG MODELS

NOTE: 'Number built' figures sometimes vary from source to source, with production numbers often differing from sales numbers. In most cases we have taken F. Wilson McComb in his book 'MG by McComb', published by Osprey, as the authority.

MODEL NAME: 14/28

PRODUCTION DETAILS: Built in Great Britain by MG
INTRODUCTION: England 1924
BODY CONFIGURATION: Two–seater open tourer, four–seater open tourer and four–door saloon versions
ENGINE: 1802cc four–cylinder, sidevalve Hotchkiss engine
TRANSMISSION: Three–speed non–synchro gearbox
PRESS COMMENTS: Morris Garages' own press advertisements claimed 'Here you have a true sporting car with an amazing performance — so flexible that it is possible to walk alongside on top gear, yet with a reserve of power that makes hill–climbing one upward, surging rush, and the speed on the level limited only by the road conditions'
SPECIAL NOTES: Based on Bullnose Morris
PRICE AT INTRODUCTION: England £350 sterling
DISCONTINUED: England 1927
NUMBER BUILT: Approximately 400

MODEL NAME: 14/40 MARK IV

PRODUCTION DETAILS: Built in Great Britain by MG
INTRODUCTION: England 1927
BODY CONFIGURATION: Two–seater and four–seater tourer, salonette, coupe and fabric covered saloon
ENGINE: 1802cc four–cylinder, sidevalve engine from Morris Oxford
TRANSMISSION: Three–speed non–synchro gearbox
PRESS COMMENTS: Promoted by Morris Garages as 'The car that takes the ills out of hills' and 'Designed and constructed by enthusiasts for enthusiasts'
SPECIAL NOTES: A development of the final, flat–radiator version of the original 14/28. Engine now claimed to produce 35bhp at 4000rpm. First model to bear the brown and beige octagon MG badge. First MG to win a motor racing event
PRICE AT INTRODUCTION: England Two–seater £340 sterling; Four–seater £350 sterling; Salonette £475 sterling
DISCONTINUED: England 1929
NUMBER BUILT: Approximately 700

MODEL NAME: MG 18/80 MARK I/II

PRODUCTION DETAILS: Built in Great Britain by MG
INTRODUCTION: England: Mark I — August 1928; Mark II — 1929
BODY CONFIGURATION: Two–seater and four–seater open tourer and saloon versions
ENGINE: 2468cc OHC six–cylinder
TRANSMISSION: Mark I — three–speed gearbox non–synchro. Mark II — Four–speed gearbox non–synchro
PRESS COMMENTS: MG Car Company advertising stated 'the customer was taken to Brooklands track by a London distributor. In spite of a rain storm which meant having the hood in position, the MG Six Sports Tourer, with no preparation at all and carrying driver and two passengers, achieved a speed of 83.5 miles per hour'
SPECIAL NOTES: Engine from Morris Six/Isis. First chassis of MG's own design. First MG to bear the Kimber designed radiator. Amy Johnson was presented with a Mark I salonette by Sir William Morris. Mark IIs were still offered from stock up to one year after production stopped. Apart from the gearbox the Mark II differed from the Mark I by having bigger brake drums and wider track
PRICE AT INTRODUCTION: England £480 to £555 sterling
DISCONTINUED: England, Mark I 1931, Mark II 1932
NUMBER BUILT: Mark I 500, Mark II 236

MODEL NAME: MG M–TYPE MIDGET

PRODUCTION DETAILS: Built in Great Britain by MG
INTRODUCTION: England, 1929
BODY CONFIGURATION: Boat–tailed two–seater sports car. Fabric body originally offered and metal panelled version later. Also sportsman's coupe with partly glass–panelled sun roof
ENGINE: 847cc OHC four–cylinder derived from Wolseley, based on Hispano–Suiza aero–engine design
TRANSMISSION: Three–speed non–synchro gearbox
PRESS COMMENTS: 'An intriguing specialized small car with a fine all–round performance.', 'Considering the diminutive engine and its propensities for revving one is not prepared to expect flexibility on top gear to any great extent ... one is promptly deceived, and in the thickest of London traffic very little gear changing is necessary.'
SPECIAL NOTES: Based on Morris Minor.
PRICE AT INTRODUCTION: England £175 sterling
DISCONTINUED: England 1932
NUMBER BUILT: 3235

MODEL NAME: MG 18/100 'TIGRESS'

PRODUCTION DETAILS: Built in Great Britain by MG
INTRODUCTION: England 1930
BODY CONFIGURATION: Four–seater tourer built for racing
ENGINE: 2468cc single overhead camshaft six–cylinder
TRANSMISSION: Four–speed manual non–synchro gearbox
PRESS COMMENTS: Car not tested by the press
SPECIAL NOTES: Based on the MG 18/80 Mark II. Engine upgraded with new crankshaft, pistons, camshaft, dry–sump lubrication, cross–flow cylinder head, and two spark plugs per cylinder
PRICE AT INTRODUCTION: England £895 sterling
DISCONTINUED: England 1931
NUMBER BUILT: 5

MODEL NAME: MG C–TYPE MIDGET

PRODUCTION DETAILS: Built in Great Britain by MG
INTRODUCTION: England 1931
BODY CONFIGURATION: Two–seater competition car

ENGINE: 746cc single OHC four–cylinder. Also available in supercharged form

TRANSMISSION: Four–speed non–synchro gearbox

PRESS COMMENTS: 'In spite of the fact that this is a proper competition car, there is nothing which makes the machine unsuitable for touring... Something close on 90mph is an amazing speed for a 750cc car that is also a practical vehicle on the road... is as steady as the proverbial rock, is comfortably sprung as well, possesses a gear change that is a delight in consistency'

SPECIAL NOTES: Known as the 'Montlhéry Midget' after the banked course near Paris where MG had set speed records. Version of original MG M–type Midget with short stroke 750cc engine

PRICE AT INTRODUCTION: England £295 sterling (£345 supercharged)

DISCONTINUED: England 1932

NUMBER BUILT: 44

MODEL NAME: MG D–TYPE MIDGET

PRODUCTION DETAILS: Built in Great Britain by MG

INTRODUCTION: England 1931

BODY CONFIGURATION: Two–door, four–seater open tourer or 'salonette' sedan

ENGINE: 847cc single OHC four–cylinder (as in M–type)

TRANSMISSION: Three–speed (four–speed optional on later models) non–synchro gearbox

PRESS COMMENTS: 'the eagerness of the engine to turn over at extremely high revs, 5800rpm being well within its capabilities... pockets in the doors, a space for small luggage in the tail, and an easily erected hood and side screens for bad weather have not been neglected'

SPECIAL NOTES: This is a version of the M–type, lengthened to four–seater body

PRICE AT INTRODUCTION: Open model £210 sterling, closed version £250

DISCONTINUED: England 1932

NUMBER BUILT: Approximately 250

MODEL NAME: MG F–TYPE MAGNA

PRODUCTION DETAILS: Built in Great Britain by MG

INTRODUCTION: England 1931

BODY CONFIGURATION: Two and four–seater open tourer, two and four–seater 'salonette'

ENGINE: 1271cc six–cylinder derived from Wolseley Hornet

TRANSMISSION: Four–speed non–synchro ENV gearbox

PRESS COMMENTS: 'The appearance of the car is extremely attractive and is enhanced by setting the radiator in a slightly sloping position. The engine is completely sealed from the driving compartment, so that there is no likelihood of fumes reaching the passengers.'

SPECIAL NOTES: Three versions: F1, F2 and F3

PRICE AT INTRODUCTION: Open four–seater £250 sterling, sliding–roof four–seater £289 sterling

DISCONTINUED: England 1932

NUMBER BUILT: Approximately 1250

MODEL NAME: MG J–TYPE MIDGET

PRODUCTION DETAILS: Built in Great Britain by MG

INTRODUCTION: England 1932

BODY CONFIGURATION: Two–seater sports and racing cars

ENGINE: J1 and J2 — 847cc OHC four–cylinder two bearing engine. J3 and J4 — 746cc supercharged OHC four–cylinder

TRANSMISSION: Four–speed non–synchro gearbox

PRESS COMMENTS: 'Getting into the J2 demands some agility; the cockpit is pretty snug and the steering wheel comes close to the chest', 'a very acceptable level of performance'

SPECIAL NOTES: J1 and J2 were sports cars. J3 and J4 were racing cars. J2 introduced what was to become the classic Midget styling

PRICE AT INTRODUCTION: J1 £199 sterling

DISCONTINUED: England J1, J3 and J4 — 1933. J2 — 1934

NUMBER BUILT: J1 380, J2 2083, J3 22, J4 9

MODEL NAME: MG K–TYPE MAGNETTE (KA & KB ENGINES)

PRODUCTION DETAILS: Built in Great Britain by MG

INTRODUCTION: England 1932

BODY CONFIGURATION: (K1) Four–seater saloon and four–seater open tourer, (K2) Two–seater tourer

ENGINE: 1087cc six–cylinder

TRANSMISSION: KA, Wilson four–speed preselector gearbox; KB, four–speed non–synchro gearbox

PRESS COMMENTS: 'A particularly interesting, high–efficiency car'. 'The overhead camshaft engine of this series is entirely new and was primarily designed for supercharging, consequently there is a very big margin of safety as produced in unsupercharged form'.

SPECIAL NOTES: KA engine had three SU carburettors, KB had two SU carburettors

PRICE AT INTRODUCTION: £445 sterling (K1 saloon), £385 sterling (K1 tourer)

DISCONTINUED: England 1933

NUMBER BUILT: (estimates) (K1) 71, (K2) 15.

MODEL NAME: MG K–TYPE MAGNETTE (KD ENGINE)

PRODUCTION DETAILS: Built in Great Britain by MG

INTRODUCTION: England 1933

BODY CONFIGURATION: (K1) Four–seater saloon and four–seater open tourer, (K2) Two–seater tourer

ENGINE: 1271cc six–cylinder

TRANSMISSION: Wilson four–speed preselector gearbox

PRESS COMMENTS: '...an excellent range of well–tried cars made even better by modifications which have been found in the light of experience to be substantial improvements'.

SPECIAL NOTES: Almost identical to the previous model Magnettes except for the larger engine and a single plate clutch now linking the engine to the preselector gearbox

PRICE AT INTRODUCTION: £445 sterling (saloon), £390 sterling (two–seater tourer)

DISCONTINUED: England 1934

NUMBER BUILT: (estimates) (K1) 80, (K2) 5.

MODEL NAME: MG K3 MAGNETTE

PRODUCTION DETAILS: Built in Great Britain by MG
INTRODUCTION: England 1932
BODY CONFIGURATION: Two–seater racing car
ENGINE: 1087cc supercharged six–cylinder
TRANSMISSION: Wilson four–speed preselector gearbox
PRESS COMMENTS: 'The K3 marked the high point in the SOHC MG engine.', 'The car's steering is truck–heavy at very low mph', 'The K3 Magnette is immense fun and excitement and a challenge to drive', 'the preselector can be shifted with extreme smoothness and good speed, the clutch taking hold positively and instantaneously with a deliciously abrupt change in exhaust note.', 'It takes some living with the device (the preselector gearbox) to feel at home with it.'
SPECIAL NOTES: Widely regarded as the best racing car MG ever made and claimed to be the most successful 1100cc racing car ever made. Formed the base for the record breaking EX135. Won its class in the 1933 Mille Miglia and won the 1933 Ulster TT
PRICE AT INTRODUCTION: £795 sterling
DISCONTINUED: England 1934
NUMBER BUILT: 33

MODEL NAME: MG MAGNA L1 AND L2

PRODUCTION DETAILS: Built in Great Britain by MG
INTRODUCTION: England 1933
BODY CONFIGURATION: Two–seater sports and coupe
ENGINE: 1087cc six–cylinder
TRANSMISSION: Four–speed non–synchro gearbox
PRESS COMMENTS: 'a piquant and intensely alive little car', 'Sitting well down in a deep cockpit rendered comfortable by pneumatic upholstery', 'the steering has no apparent vices', 'One of the features is the four–speed twin–top gear box with remote–control.', 'The ratios are well chosen and the car will reach 40mph on second gear', 'the open two–seater Magna is a most delectable car with the manners, as well as the air, of a thorough-bred.'
SPECIAL NOTES: Body design of the L2 was very similar to that on the F2 and J2 cars, except for stylishly swept front guards similar to those on the K2
PRICE AT INTRODUCTION: From £285 to £345 sterling
DISCONTINUED: England 1934
NUMBER BUILT: L1 486, L2 90

MODEL NAME: MG N–TYPE

PRODUCTION DETAILS: Built in Great Britain by MG
INTRODUCTION: England, NA — 1934. NB — 1936. NE — 1934
BODY CONFIGURATION: NA and NB — two–door sports and tourer with smooth tail and built in petrol tank. ND — Simpler two–seater with slab tank using left over K2 bodies. NE — two–seater competition car
ENGINE: 1271cc OHC six–cylinder engine, which was a further development of the KN engine.
TRANSMISSION: Four–speed non synchro gearbox
PRESS COMMENTS: 'It is not just that the car is fast... it is that it feels so very much better.', 'This engine seems veritably to delight in revs, yet it remains delightfully smooth and quiet', 'it should be capable of giving as high a speed as 80mph.' It is a sports car, yet it is not harsh in its riding'
SPECIAL NOTES: NB differed from NA having lower scuttle and front hinged doors. NE developed for 1934 Ulster Tourist Trophy, four of the six entries retiring, one finishing well down the field and the sixth winning the prestigious event. NB was the last OHC small six MG
PRICE AT INTRODUCTION: NA — £305 sterling. NB — £280 sterling
DISCONTINUED: England NA — 1935; NB and NE — 1934
NUMBER BUILT: NA and NB — 690. ND — 48. NE — 7

MODEL NAME: MG P–TYPE

PRODUCTION DETAILS: Built in Great Britain by MG
INTRODUCTION: England, PA — 1934, PB — 1935
BODY CONFIGURATION: Two or four–seater sports or tourer. Also Airline Coupe
ENGINE: PA — 847cc OHC four–cylinder three bearing engine. PB — 939cc OHC four–cylinder three bearing engine
TRANSMISSION: Four–speed non–synchromesh gearbox
PRESS COMMENTS: 'The suspension is very good ... comfort over long and fast runs is an outstanding characteristic.', 'One of the most pleasing aspects is the top gear performance', 'Gear change is a real delight', 'the rev counter will climb... 5500rpm... with a smooth silkiness that tempts overmuch work with the neat gear lever.', ' an unusually attractive sports model with an outstanding performance.'
SPECIAL NOTES: Brake drums larger than J–type. Third centre bearing in crankshaft compared to J–type's two. PB had different dash layout and slatted radiator compared with PA. PB was last OHC Midget
PRICE AT INTRODUCTION: £222 sterling
DISCONTINUED: England 1936
NUMBER BUILT: PA — 1973. PB — 526. Airline coupes — Fewer than 50

MODEL NAME: MG KN

PRODUCTION DETAILS: Built in Great Britain by MG
INTRODUCTION: England 1934
BODY CONFIGURATION: Saloon body only
ENGINE: 1271cc OHC six–cylinder
TRANSMISSION: Four–speed, non–synchromesh gearbox
PRESS COMMENTS: 'The engine is the N–type', ' has all the typical MG roadworthiness and fast performance, but offers the comfort of a roomy saloon body.', 'very graceful and well proportioned', ' runs quietly and easily, and is very pleasant to handle.'
SPECIAL NOTES: KN is a K1 (long) chassis with the N–type engine (which was a further–developed KD engine).
PRICE AT INTRODUCTION: £399 sterling
DISCONTINUED: England 1935
NUMBER BUILT: 201

MODEL NAME: MG QA

PRODUCTION DETAILS: Built in Great Britain by MG
INTRODUCTION: England 1934
BODY CONFIGURATION: Two–seater competition car
ENGINE: 746cc supercharged OHC four–cylinder
TRANSMISSION: Pre–selector four–speed gearbox with overload clutch
PRESS COMMENTS: 'The car has lapped Brooklands at 111mph and is capable of exceeding 120mph on a straightaway.', 'wheelbase is considerably longer than that of the ordinary MG Midget', 'develops its high power output at a speed of 7300rpm', 'chassis frame is of underslung design'
SPECIAL NOTES: Top speed of 120mph was later considered by some critics as too fast for this chassis
PRICE AT INTRODUCTION: £550 sterling
DISCONTINUED: England 1934
NUMBER BUILT: 8

MODEL NAME: MG RA

PRODUCTION DETAILS: Built in Great Britain by MG
INTRODUCTION: England 1935
BODY CONFIGURATION: Single–seater racing car
ENGINE: 746cc supercharged OHC four–cylinder
TRANSMISSION: Four–speed preselector gearbox
PRESS COMMENTS: 'Definitely it departs from convention', 'The brakes are extraordinarily good... and so powerful that you have to be quite careful not to push hard on the pedal', 'The steering... a bit too stiff at the moment for the average road circuit'
SPECIAL NOTES: MG's only single–seater racing car. Q series engine with new stronger backbone chassis with fully–independent wishbone and torsion bar suspension on all four wheels. Body streamlined like German Grand Prix cars of the day. Won 750cc class in 1935 French Grand Prix. The last of the purely racing MG Midgets
PRICE AT INTRODUCTION: £750 in GB
DISCONTINUED: England 1935
NUMBER BUILT: 10

MODEL NAME: MG SA

PRODUCTION DETAILS: Built in Great Britain by MG
INTRODUCTION: England 1936
BODY CONFIGURATION: Four–door saloon, drophead coupe
ENGINE: 2288cc, later 2322cc OHV six–cylinder
TRANSMISSION: Four–speed , synchromesh on third and fourth gears
PRESS COMMENTS: 'Speed with silence', 'Quite the handsomest production ever built by the MG concern', 'The engine is not tuned to a fine edge of performance which will call for constant attention', 'The remarkably low price of the complete saloon at £375 ... will bring this model within the reach of thousands of enthusiasts'
SPECIAL NOTES: Designed to supersede the KN saloon
PRICE AT INTRODUCTION: £375 sterling
DISCONTINUED: England 1939
NUMBER BUILT: 2738

MODEL NAME: MG TA

PRODUCTION DETAILS: Built in Great Britain by MG
INTRODUCTION: 1936
BODY CONFIGURATION: Two–door sports, Airline coupe and drophead coupe
ENGINE: 1292cc OHV four–cylinder
TRANSMISSION: Four–speed manual, remote central control
PRESS COMMENTS: 'The car has trim lines, a very low and sturdy frame (underslung at the back) and comfort-able provision for two people', 'Lockheed hydraulic type brakes are used instead of the cable–operated pattern on former MG Midgets', 'The longer wheelbase has rendered a very generous luggage compartment possible'
SPECIAL NOTES: Introduced as the 'Series T', the car became known as the TA only in retrospect as TB, TC, etc models were released
PRICE AT INTRODUCTION: £222 sterling
DISCONTINUED: England 1939
NUMBER BUILT: 3003

MODEL NAME: MG VA OR 1½–LITRE

PRODUCTION DETAILS: Built in Great Britain by MG
INTRODUCTION: England 1937
BODY CONFIGURATION: Saloon, four–seater sports and drophead coupe
ENGINE: 1548cc four–cylinder
TRANSMISSION: Four–speed gearbox with synchromesh on 2nd, 3rd and 4th
PRESS COMMENTS: 'Attractive model with wide appeal', 'Brisk performance, good steering and untiring to drive on long journeys', 'Shock absorbing is effected by means of a Luvax hydraulic system... the tension can be varied from the dashboard to suit road and speed conditions', 'There is an air of refinement throughout the entire car'
SPECIAL NOTES: Designed to fill the gap between the T–Series Midget and the 2–litre SA models
PRICE AT INTRODUCTION: £280 sterling
DISCONTINUED: England 1939
NUMBER BUILT: About 2407

MODEL NAME: MG WA OR 2.6–LITRE

PRODUCTION DETAILS: Built in Great Britain by MG
INTRODUCTION: 1938
BODY CONFIGURATION: Saloon, four–seater sports and drophead coupe
ENGINE: 2561cc OHV six–cylinder
TRANSMISSION: Four–speed gearbox with synchromesh on top three gears
PRESS COMMENTS: 'High performance engine in an improved type of chassis carrying more capacious coachwork', 'Appearance is characterised by a very long bonnet with an almost horizontal top line', 'Draughtless ventilation is provided by hinged triangular glass panels in the windows of the doors'
SPECIAL NOTES: The WA engine had its oil passed via coiled copper pipe within the water jacket to provide rapid warming from cold and cooling during hard driving
PRICE AT INTRODUCTION: £442 sterling
DISCONTINUED: England 1939
NUMBER BUILT: 369

MODEL NAME: MG TB

PRODUCTION DETAILS: Built in Great Britain by MG
INTRODUCTION: England 1939
BODY CONFIGURATION: Two–door sports and drophead coupe
ENGINE: 1250cc OHV four–cylinder XPAG unit, derived from Morris Ten
TRANSMISSION: Four–speed gearbox with synchromesh on top three gears
PRESS COMMENTS: 'With higher powered short stroke engine and with improved gearbox synchronised on upper three speeds', 'The crankshaft is now counterbalanced... being fed with oil at high pressure from the aluminium alloy sump', 'Has a maximum speed in the vicinity of 80mph', 'Improved lighting equipment'
SPECIAL NOTES: Chassis and body unchanged from original T–Series (now known as TA). Larger bore and shorter stroke gave slightly smaller capacity but increased output by two horsepower. Clutch and gearbox also improved
PRICE AT INTRODUCTION: £225 sterling
DISCONTINUED: England 1939
NUMBER BUILT: 379

MODEL NAME: MG TC

PRODUCTION DETAILS: Built in Great Britain by MG
INTRODUCTION: England 1945, Australia 1946
BODY CONFIGURATION: Two–door sports
ENGINE: 1250cc OHV four–cylinder XPAG
TRANSMISSION: Four–speed gearbox with no synchro on first
PRESS COMMENTS: 'Although the front and rear track remain the same, the body is four inches wider across the seats than the TB', 'Semi–elliptical springs are now fitted with shackles at their trailing ends, rather than the sliding trunnions of the TA and TB', 'The engine is very quick to respond to the throttle pedal', 'The adjustable steering wheel requires less than two turns from lock to lock'
SPECIAL NOTES: First MG to sell in large numbers overseas (especially the USA). Prince Philip owned one. Virtually identical to TB but with slightly wider body.
PRICE AT INTRODUCTION: England £480 sterling, Australia £695.
DISCONTINUED: England and Australia 1949
NUMBER BUILT: 10,000. Of these, 6493 were export sales including 2000 to the USA

MODEL NAME: MG Y

PRODUCTION DETAILS: Built in Great Britain by MG
INTRODUCTION: England 1947, Australia 1947
BODY CONFIGURATION: Four–door sedan and four–seater open tourer
ENGINE: 1250cc OHV four–cylinder
TRANSMISSION: Four–speed gearbox, no synchro on first
PRESS COMMENTS: 'New independently sprung model from a famous sports car factory', 'There is an initial impression that the car's performance is relatively indifferent... when the performance is checked by the stopwatch... the figures obtained are outstanding for a luxurious 11 HP saloon'

SPECIAL NOTES: First production MG with independent front suspension. Open four–seater tourer YT introduced in 1949 and intended for export only
PRICE AT INTRODUCTION: England £672 sterling, Australia n/a
DISCONTINUED: England 1953, Australia 1953
NUMBER BUILT: YA 6158, YB 1301, YT 877

MODEL NAME: MG TD

PRODUCTION DETAILS: Built in Great Britain by MG
INTRODUCTION: TD — England 1949, Australia 1950; TD MkII — England 1952, Australia 1952
BODY CONFIGURATION: Two–door sports
ENGINE: 1250cc OHV four–cylinder
TRANSMISSION: Four–speed gearbox, no synchromesh on first
PRESS COMMENTS: '...amazing increase in comfort brought about by the adoption of the independent suspension.', 'maximum comforts combined with economical running.', 'a real sports car at a price within the range of the average enthusiast.'
SPECIAL NOTES: TD was first MG sports car with independent front suspension and MG's first best seller in America. TD MkIIA was a competition version. First MG sold with left–hand drive version
PRICE AT INTRODUCTION: England £569 sterling, Australia £900
DISCONTINUED: England and Australia, TD — 1952, TD MkII — 1953
NUMBER BUILT: TD and TD MkII — 29,664. TD MkIIA — 47

MODEL NAME: MG TF

PRODUCTION DETAILS: Built in Great Britain by MG
INTRODUCTION: England 1953, Australia 1954
BODY CONFIGURATION: Two–door sports
ENGINE: 1953–54 — 1250cc OHV four–cylinder XPAG engine. 1955 — 1466cc OHV four–cylinder XPEG engine
TRANSMISSION: Four–speed gearbox with no synchro on first
PRESS COMMENTS: 'A certain amount of modernisation has taken place', 'lower frontal area than the TD', 'Power output has been increased from 54.5bhp to 57.5bhp', 'not until 2500rpm does the power really take hold', 'The pull–type starter is very unhandy', 'still the greatest sports car for the money available today'
SPECIAL NOTES: The TF was a quickly developed stop gap to replace the aging TD when BMC management failed to approve EX175 (MGA) for production
PRICE AT INTRODUCTION: England £780 sterling, Australia £982
DISCONTINUED: England and Australia 1955
NUMBER BUILT: 1250cc — 6200. 1466cc –3400

MODEL NAME: MG ZA & ZB MAGNETTE

PRODUCTION DETAILS: Built in Great Britain by MG
INTRODUCTION: England 1953, Australia 1954
BODY CONFIGURATION: Four–door saloon only
ENGINE: 1489cc OHV four–cylinder BMC

TRANSMISSION: Four–speed gearbox with no synchro in first

PRESS COMMENTS: 'A pleasant picture for those motorists who require a lively saloon which can provide comfort while possessing a sporting character', 'the engine is willing to work hard and is very smooth', 'The engine's cheerful ability to rev is matched by the roadholding of the car, which is remarkable indeed', 'a tall man does not feel cramped after a long fast journey'

SPECIAL NOTES: The ZA Magnette received the BMC 1500 engine while the TF, introduced at the same time, retained a developed version of the old XPAG 1250 and had to wait another year for its 1466cc engine

PRICE AT INTRODUCTION: England £915 sterling, Australia £1285

DISCONTINUED: England 1958, Australia 1959

NUMBER BUILT: ZA 12,754; ZB 23,846

MODEL NAME: MGA 1500 AND 1600

PRODUCTION DETAILS: Built in Great Britain by MG. Assembled in Australia by Nuffield Distributors Ltd, Joynton Ave, Zetland, with imported mechanicals from 1960 to 1962. Tyres, batteries and some items of trim were locally supplied when the MGA was first assembled. Some models, like coupes and Twin Cam, were imported

INTRODUCTION: England 1955, Australia 1956

BODY CONFIGURATION: Two–door, two–seater sports or coupe

ENGINE: 1956–59 1489cc four–cylinder B series engine (tuned version of the Magnette sedan's). 1959–60 — Twin cam 1600cc engine available. 1959–61 — 1588cc (1600 MkI) engine. 1961–62 — 1622cc (1600 MkII) engine

TRANSMISSION: Four–speed gearbox with no synchro in first

PRESS COMMENTS: 'To drive the MGA on a winding road is an enthusiast's delight', 'The cornering power of the car is extremely good.', 'An uncommonly roadworthy 1.5–litre sports car of high performance', 'Faster, with more torque for hill climbing and acceleration, the latest MGA 1600 now offers much more pleasing performance than the earlier 1500.'

SPECIAL NOTES: First totally new MG since before WW2. First MG with all–enveloping bodywork. Designed by Syd Enever. Front suspension was the only mechanical component carried over from the MG TF. Four–wheel Dunlop disc brakes were standard with the twin–cam engine but were also available on the De–Luxe pushrod versions built as a special order between 1961 and 1962. These are the rarest MGAs of all. 1955–1961 — Flush grille. 1962 — Recessed grille

PRICE AT INTRODUCTION: England £844 sterling, Australia £1147

DISCONTINUED: England 1962, Australia 1962

NUMBER BUILT: 1500 58,750; Twin Cam 2111; 1600 MkI 31,501; 1600 MkII 8719

MODEL NAME: MG MAGNETTE MKIII AND MKIV

PRODUCTION DETAILS: Built in Great Britain by MG

INTRODUCTION: England, MkIII 1959, MkIV 1961

BODY CONFIGURATION: Four–door saloon only

ENGINE: MkIII 1489cc OHV four–cylinder, MkIV 1622cc OHV four–cylinder

TRANSMISSION: Four–speed with no synchromesh on first, optional automatic on MkIV

PRESS COMMENTS: 'Well appointed, Farina–styled sports saloon', 'Magnette enthusiasts will be pleased to find that seats similar to those on the previous model are fitted', 'In layout, the new Magnette is quite conventional', 'the car suffered from marked roll oversteer'

SPECIAL NOTES: Badge engineered Farina–styled Austin A55/Morris Oxford

PRICE AT INTRODUCTION: England £1072 sterling

DISCONTINUED: England 1968

NUMBER BUILT: MkIII 15,676; MkIV 13,738

MODEL NAME: MG MIDGET MKI, MKII, MKIII

PRODUCTION DETAILS: Built in Great Britain by MG

INTRODUCTION: England 1961, Australia 1968 (sold in Austin–Healey Sprite form until that date)

BODY CONFIGURATION: Two–door, two–seater sports car

ENGINE: Initially available with 948cc A series four–cylinder engine then later with 1098cc four–cylinder engine. 1966 MkIII — 1275cc four–cylinder engine. 1974 MkIII — 1493cc four–cylinder Triumph engine

TRANSMISSION: Four–speed with no synchromesh on first

PRESS COMMENTS: 'The Midget impressed us with its performance and handling and ... is not an overpriced car. But it still lacks a lot in comfort (the cockpit is far too small for tall drivers).'

SPECIAL NOTES: Badge engineered Austin–Healey Sprite. First MG since 1936 to have an engine of less than 1–litre

PRICE AT INTRODUCTION: England £670 sterling, Australia (1968) $2480

DISCONTINUED: England 1979, Australia 1972

NUMBER BUILT: GAN1 — 16,080; GAN2 — 9601; GAN3 — 26,601; GAN4 — 13,722; GAN5 — 86,650; GAN6 — 72,185. Last 500 cars in UK finished completely in black

MODEL NAME: MGB MKI AND MKII

PRODUCTION DETAILS: Built in Great Britain by MG, 1962 to 1980. Assembled in Australia by BMC from April 1963 and then by Leyland Australia from 1970 to 1972. When production stopped local content was up to 45 percent

INTRODUCTION: England MkI — 1962, MkII — 1967; Australia MkI — April 1963. MkII — 1969; MGBL — July 1970

BODY CONFIGURATION: Two–door, two–seater, sports car; 1965 — GT coupe version; 1970 — Recessed black grille; 1974 — US spec impact resistant bumpers adopted

ENGINE: 1798cc version of BMC B series OHV four–cylinder, three main–bearing engine. Five main–bearing engine adopted in 1964

TRANSMISSION: Four–speed all–synchro gearbox. 1968 — Overdrive on third and fourth gear and automatic available. 1970 MGBL — Three–speed Borg–Warner 35 automatic transmission optional

PRESS COMMENTS: 'A contemporary mixture of grand tourer with sports car lines', 'quick and precise steering, oversize brakes, and a generous power reserve.', 'The sort of car you can enjoy driving solo', 'The sad fact is that the later MGBs were no faster, but considerably heavier than the original models... and the handling certainly wasn't as good as it was before the entire shell was raised on its suspension in the mid–1970s.'; GT — 'an absolute delight', 'new standards for medium–priced grand touring automobiles.'

SPECIAL NOTES: The most successful MG ever built. Styled by Don Hayter

PRICE AT INTRODUCTION: England, MkI — £950 sterling; Australia, MkI — £1356; MkII — $3195, MkII with Overdrive — $3325. MGBL — $3560

DISCONTINUED: England, MkI 1967, MkII 1980; Australia, MkI — 1968. MkII — 1970. MGBL — November 1972. Private imports after 1972

NUMBER BUILT: GHN3 — 115,808; GHD3 — 21,835; GHN4&5 — 271,361; GHD4&5 — 103,786 (includes GTs). Last 1000 cars were special Limited Edition models

MODEL NAME: MG 1100 & MG 1300

PRODUCTION DETAILS: Built in Great Britain by MG

INTRODUCTION: England 1962; Australia, privately imported only

BODY CONFIGURATION: Two–door and four–door saloons

ENGINE: 1098cc OHV four–cylinder (1100) and 1275cc OHV four–cylinder (1300)

TRANSMISSION: Four–speed gearbox, no synchromesh on first (all–synchromesh from 1968)

SPECIAL NOTES: Badge–engineered version of Morris 1100 saloon

PRICE AT INTRODUCTION: England £812 sterling

DISCONTINUED: England 1971

NUMBER BUILT: 1100 — 116,827; 1300 — 26,240

MODEL NAME: MGC

PRODUCTION DETAILS: Built in Great Britain by MG

INTRODUCTION: England 1967; Australia, privately imported only

BODY CONFIGURATION: Two–door, two–seater sports and GT coupe

ENGINE: 2.9–litre OHV six–cylinder

TRANSMISSION: Four–speed manual, all–synchromesh

PRESS COMMENTS: 'One of the worst cars I have ever driven' (Stirling Moss). 'A haphazard parentage', 'the engine itself was a venerable design, in need of either total redesign or at least updating.', 'The engine is quiet ... and noticeably smoother [than the Healey] but a noisy cooling fan is prominent. Fuel economy isn't especially good at 17.8mpg.'

SPECIAL NOTES: Torsion bar front suspension because trimming the front MGB crossmember to allow the longer engine to pass over it would leave insufficient structure for coil springs. Front suspension and cross member had to be redesigned

PRICE AT INTRODUCTION: England £1112 sterling

DISCONTINUED: England 1969

NUMBER BUILT: Roadsters — 4542, GTs — 4457

MODEL NAME: MGB GT V8

PRODUCTION DETAILS: Built in Great Britain by MG

INTRODUCTION: England 1972. Australia, privately imported only

BODY CONFIGURATION: Two–door GT coupe

ENGINE: 3528cc Rover OHV V8. 40lbs lighter than 1798cc four–cylinder

TRANSMISSION: Four–speed gearbox, all–synchromesh

PRESS COMMENTS: 'truly exciting performance... much better fuel economy and handling than the MGC.', 'Smooth, flexible engine; well–chosen gear ratios and overdrive; roomy for two; good visibility. Poor low–speed ride; haphazard instruments and controls; dated decor; high wind noise at speed; rather expensive.'

SPECIAL NOTES: The final development of the original MGB, which had survived in various forms for almost two decades before being discontinued. Chassis numbers 101 through 2903 were MGB GT V8s. First rubber bumper GT V8 was number 2101. Chassis number 1957 to 2100, and 2633 to 2700 were not used and do not exist.

PRICE AT INTRODUCTION: England £2294 sterling

DISCONTINUED: England 1976

NUMBER BUILT: 2591

MODEL NAME: MG RV8

PRODUCTION DETAILS: Built in Cowley, Great Britain by Rover–MG

INTRODUCTION: England 1993. Australia (to be decided)

BODY CONFIGURATION: Two–door sports roadster

ENGINE: 3946cc (94.0 x 71.12 mm) Rover OHV V8 with Lucas multi–point electronic fuel–injection

TRANSMISSION: Five–speed manual, all–synchromesh, LT77

SPECIAL COMMENTS: (by John Thornley, in a letter to Peter Kerr dated November 17, 1992): "Having seen the MG RV8, I can say three things: 1) I am very pleased, because it shows that Rover now recognise... MG is the name for sports cars. 2) Quite clearly, the people responsible for it know what they are doing. I don't think it would be pompous or patronising to say that Abingdon would have been proud of it. 3) It is a pity that this up–market vehicle has had to precede the 'tiddler' — which, we understand, has now gone on the back burner for obvious reasons."

PRICE AT INTRODUCTION: England £26,500 sterling

NUMBER BUILT: (current model)

This page: In 1929 Cecil Kimber decided that the smallest Morris production car, the Minor, was an ideal base for a low–cost sports two–seater. In mid–1929, the M–Type was launched to immediate acclaim. One of 3235 M–types built, this car came here in chassis form and a local body was fitted. In later years it was converted to a beach buggy and allowed to badly deteriorate. The M–type was restored over a four–year period by Ian Heather Jnr and Ian Heather Snr.

The purposeful–looking C–type, built in 1931/2, had the characteristic MG grille replaced with an aerodynamic cowl and was known as the Montlhéry Midget. It was on the Montlhéry track in France that George Eyston became first to officially clock 100 miles per hour (162km/h) driving a car with a 750cc engine. On his first attempt using a standard radiator, Eyston failed to hit the magic 'ton' so a streamlined cowl was fashioned from an old oil drum. Eyston then clocked 103.13mph. In all, 44 C–types were built for racing.

The N–type Magnette followed the K–type, as the marque's six–cylinder offering. A total of 690 two–seater and four–seater tourers and a handful of Airline Coupes were made between 1934 and 1936, plus seven racing models. The four–seater tourer is shown here.

Remarkable Performance of the M.G. Midget

80 miles an hour and 45 miles per gallon

By J. O. Sherwood

One of the most famous cars in racing and competition overseas, the M.G. has until recently been only a sort of myth in the minds of local car enthusiasts, for,, for some surprising reason these cars have not been represented on the Australian market, and their wonderful performances could only be read of and wondered at, but not actually demonstrated in the "flesh." It was therefore with great and unusual interest that the test of the latest M.G.—stocks of which are now available to the Australian public—was carried out.

It is always a refreshing experience to change over from the everyday sort of sedan or tourer, to a piquant and intensively alive little car, and such was my feeling after having taken over the wheel of the M.G. "J2."

In a car such as this, the road is no longer a mere highway from place to place, but a path of adventure, as the sea must be to the man who handles a trim sailing craft. There is appeal in the very lines of the M.G., with its long bonnet promising speed, its workmanlike stern view, and very low driving position. To ensure the appeal, and try the car is to appreciate in full the very real qualities which are there.

This modern 4 cylinder 847 c.c. engine in the M.G. "J2" is of fine design, and it runs with notable smoothness, right throughout its range, from a comfortable toddle on top gear right up to over 5,000 revs. per minute when all out.

Its flexibility and its freedom from vibration or mechanical noise are remarkable when taken in conjunction with a big power output in relation to its size. It responds instantly to the movements of the accelerator pedal, and as the acceleration figures show, maintains its liveliness right up through the speed range. The car can be depended upon to reach its maximum on the level without hesitation.

There is a great fascination in driving the M.G. The steering is light and quick—at first grasp disconcertingly so —with a strong castor action, but, as

ROAD PERFORMANCES
Flying Half Mile—22 2/5 secs.
80.3 m.p.h.
Accelerated Half Mile—33 4/5s.
Accelerated Quarter Mile—19 2/5s
10 m.p.h. to 50 m.p.h. in top— 28 2/5s.
Slow running in top—7.2 m.p.h.
Braking to Standstill—30ft. 6in. from 30 m.p.h.
Petrol Consumption—45 m.p.g.
Maximum Speed in Gears—1st 22 m.p.h., 2nd 42 m.p.h. 3rd 62 m.p.h., top, 83 m.p.h.

soon as it is realised that the wheel held with a light grip, the car can be placed neatly, or taken round curve at speed, in an elegant fashion.

Because of the low build and speci form of spring anchorages, the ca holds the road excellently, and can be driven anywhere with confidence, with out the feeling that one is aboard small car.

One of the features is the four spee gear box, with remote control. A lo extension on the top of the box brin a short gear lever close to the hand, an the gear change is a simple and effec ive one to handle, whilst the indire gears are quiet. The ratios are ve well chosen, and the car will excee 40 m.p.h. in second gear, and 60 in thi which is pretty useful.

The clutch is sweet and light and well up to its work. It may be note that the cockpit of this car does n become hot or stuffy, for the inside sealed from the engine by rubbe around the clutch pit and also the stee ing column, which prevents hot a from blowing through.

Good Brakes.

Another point which contributes to the general attractiveness of the car is that the brakes are smooth and progressive, and may be used to pull the car up from high speed without trepidation. Because of the smoothness, they are deceptive in that they pull the car up more quickly than they appear to do, which is always a hall mark of good brakes. In the actual braking test, from 40 m.p.h., the car was pulled up smartly in 30 feet 6 inches.   Except at low speeds, when the shock absorbers can be felt to be doing their work, the comfort of riding is very good, and the ability of any car at any speed of which it is capable, is all that could be desired.

Against the Clock.

The actual figures clocked by the readers may receive the impression that a high priced super sports car is under review, and not an absolutely standard 8 h.p. Midget, the lowest priced of the extensive M.G. range. It seems nothing short of remarkable that a diminutive car of this type can amble along quietly in top gear at 8 m.p.h., then with only the pressing of the throttle accelerate in grand style without fuss or bother

right up to near its limit of 80 m.p.h., within a mile, a performance of which a car powered with an engine three times its size would be proud.

Genuine 80 m.p.h.

Two runs were made over the flying half mile, the first time in the wet when 23 1/5 secs., was clocked, equal to an average of 77.58 miles an hour. Thirty minutes later another attempt was made, this time when the road was dry, and with a slightly higher pressure on the rear tyres, the improvement in time being 4/5 secs., which brought

the average up to the rather surprising speed of 80.3 m.p.h.!

These figures indicate definitely that a standard M.G. Midget performs right up to the maker's claims of 80 m.p.h.

Acceleration through the gears is also in keeping with the car's speed capabilities, the half mile from a standing start being covered in 33 4/5 secs., and the quarter mile in 19 2/5 secs., times which very few cars of any size or make can equal. The half mile run was

finished at 74 m.p.h., and the quarter at just over 65 m.p.h.

For an eight horse power car, its top gear flexibility is quite good, although naturally not comparable with a higher powered six cylinder car.   Over a 220 yards course, the M.G. idled along at 7.4 m.p.h., average in top, from 10 m.p.h., it accelerated smartly away over a quarter mile in the same gear in 28 2/5 secs., finishing at 50 m.p.h.

Petrol Economy.

Petrol consumption affords yet another surprise for the average worked out at 45 m.p.g. It must be stated that this result was gained on a measured half gallon only, on the homeward run from the speed tests, and at an average speed of 35 m.p.h., but without taking in any very fast driving. In a private owner's hands under average condition of mixed fast and slow speeds, the Midget should exceed a good 45 m.p.g.

In reviewing this test of the M.G. one cannot but be impressed with the absolute remarkable all round ability of the car. One has to drive to actually realise its true worth, and having done so, the motto of the makers becomes firmly imbedded in one's mind "Safety fast—the car with the racing pedigree."

The chassis layout of the remarkable M.G. "J2".
Points worth noting are: Remote gear control, twin fuel lines, grouped greasing nipples on side of scuttle, underslung chassis frame at rear. upswept at front, long steering rake (adjustable), twin semi-downdraft carburettors.

In the mid–1930s, MG decided to move into the larger field and produced the SA series with a 2.3–litre engine and available with coupe, sedan and touring bodies. They were noted for a stylish appearance, low noise level and good riding comfort. The design represented excellent value and about 2700 were sold between 1936 and 1940.

This page and opposite: Some 33 supercharged versions of the Magnette were built for the 1933/34 racing season. Called K3s, they had 1.1–litre, six–cylinder engines developed in conjunction with the four–cylinder derivative, which powered the P, Q, and R series MGs. In the 1933 Mille Miglia, their first outing, a team of K3s won the class and team awards. The great Italian grand prix driver, Tazio Nuvolari, then drove one to victory in the 1933 Ulster TT. Many more successes followed. One — now on display at the National Motor Museum in Birdwood, South Australia — was raced in Europe by Prince Bira of Thailand and came here to be driven by Lord Waleran in the Australian Grand Prix. The car pictured is K3 004, owned in the UK in 1936 and 1937 by 1930s big band leader Billy Cotton. The car was awarded a Brooklands badge for a 120mph lap on 17th May, 1937. It was one of seven K3s in Australia in 1994.

Above: A 1929 model M–type MG fully restored and registered with the Vintage Sports Car Club of Australia.

Maroubra Speedway in the suburbs of Sydney in 1933. Ron Mackellar's MG tries to round up a trio of cars led by two Austin Specials.

Another Maroubra Speedway shot. Ron Mackellar's MG can be seen here, fifth from left, lined up against S. Higginson (Wolseley Hornet), O. Hirschel (Austin), Bill Conoulty (Austin), B. Shepherd (Wolseley Hornet), Charlie East (Austin) and John Sherwood (Wolseley Hornet).

John Summers planted his L–type MG Magna firmly in a ditch during the 1934 Australian Grand Prix at Phillip Island. He was fortunate enough to walk away from the accident.

A signwriter puts the finishing touches to Bill Thompson's super-charged MG K3 before the 1934 Australian Grand Prix at Phillip Island. Thompson started last in the 21–car race and missed out by only 24 seconds on catching Bob Lea–Wright's Singer for the win. The MG set fastest time for the race, 22m 11s faster than the second fastest finisher over the 206 miles (331.5 km) distance.

Yet another angle on Ron Mackellar's MG racing at Sydney's Maroubra Speedway. From the John Sherwood collection, this photo has been captioned as being taken in 1934.

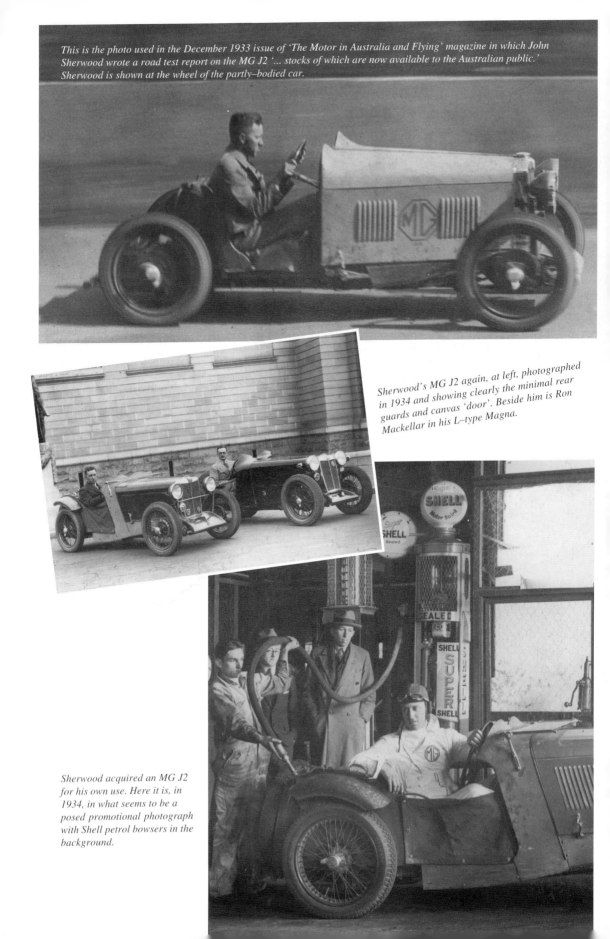

This is the photo used in the December 1933 issue of 'The Motor in Australia and Flying' magazine in which John Sherwood wrote a road test report on the MG J2 '... stocks of which are now available to the Australian public.' Sherwood is shown at the wheel of the partly–bodied car.

Sherwood's MG J2 again, at left, photographed in 1934 and showing clearly the minimal rear guards and canvas 'door'. Beside him is Ron Mackellar in his L–type Magna.

Sherwood acquired an MG J2 for his own use. Here it is, in 1934, in what seems to be a posed promotional photograph with Shell petrol bowsers in the background.

Jack Clements in this J–type MG, starting 35 minutes ahead of the scratch man, led the 1934 Australian Grand Prix at Phillip Island for much of its distance, finally finishing in third place.

Captioned simply 'Newcastle 1934' this photo depicts a very smart–looking MG ready for a road trial.

Les Jennings in his stripped L–type Magna ready for the Phillip Island Australian Grand Prix in 1934. He finished fourth outright and set second fastest race time.

Another MG at Phillip Island in 1934. The lack of a racing number suggests the photo might have been taken during practice and makes the car difficult to identify. Our calculated guess is that it is the L–type Magna of R Anderson.

A team of three MG J2s at Phillip Island for the 1934 LCCA Winter 100. Colin Keefer and Ted Martin with car 18, Jim Skinner and unknown mechanic with car 19, and Jack Clements with car 20. Car 18 survived and in the 1990s was in the hands of Ron Kilcullen in West Australia.

'Jim Fagan (Magnette K3) Phillip Island' the original hand–written caption says. Bill Thompson raced this car at Phillip Island in the 1934 and 1935 AGPs, so this was probably taken in late 1935 after K3 002 was sold to Fagan. Fagan also raced the car in the Victor Harbor AGP late in 1936.

Above: Another shot from the same, late 1935 Phillip Island meeting. Cec Warren (in dark jumper and white trousers) attends to his Q–type MG on its '... first appearance in Australia'.

Hope Bartlett had been one of the stars of racing at the old Maroubra Speedway in Bugattis but a move to this J2 MG in the mid–1930s proved to be less successful.

The Q–type MG was more successful for Hope Bartlett in the late–1930s. He drove it in reliability trials, hillclimbs and on race circuits.

Above: Les Murphy won the 1936 Australian Grand Prix, held on Boxing Day of that year, with this P–type MG. Murphy set sixth fastest time for the race distance on his way to handicap victory.

The R–type MG, only 10 of which were built in 1935, was a pure racing car and the first MG to have fully independent suspension on all four wheels. None came to Australia at that time, although a keen Australian collector has imported an example in recent years.

John Sherwood took over driving Alan Crago's stripped MG TA during a pit stop on lap 19 in the first race at Bathurst, the 1938 Australian Grand Prix, run on a dirt surface. Sherwood finished in third place.

Another angle on the Alan Crago MG TA driven to third place in the 1938 Australian Grand Prix at Bathurst by John Sherwood. The TA first appeared in England in 1936 but no examples of the model were raced in Australia until 1937.

Australian Grand Prix at Bathurst in 1938, Jim Fagan at the wheel of his supercharged MG K3 Magnette. Raced in Europe in 1933 by such luminaries as Tim Birkin, Bernard Rubin, Kaye Don and Eddie Hall, this car was twice second in the Australian Grand Prix in the hands of Bill Thompson, before being sold to Fagan. It was later raced by Ken Tubman and in the 1990s was in the hands of Adam Berryman of Victoria.

Colin Dunne finished second in the South Australian Grand Prix and the Lobethal 50 Mile Race in 1938 with this ex–Prince Bira MG K3. The car was raced post–WW2 by Ron Uffindel before being sold to Lex Davison, for whom John Barraclough drove the car in 1949 and 1950.

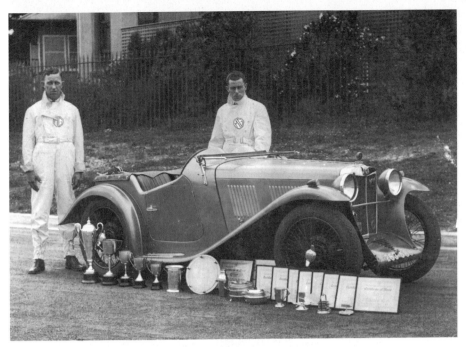

Obviously successful was this MG J2 trials car of John Sherwood and George Barton, judging by the array of trophies. The J2 in England was the first MG to have swept–back front mudguards. This car looks different, from the scuttle back, compared to English–bodied cars, and the doors hinge at the front instead of at the rear.

1933 Early L Type, 6 cylinder Magna MG.

A J3 MG scrambles up Rob Roy Hillclimb in the 1930s. This particular car is fitted with full road gear, including mud-guards and headlights, and sports two 'aero' windscreens.

Above: Parramatta Park practice day, 1938. John Sherwood at the wheel of his 'TT' NE Magnette. These cars were produced for the 1934 Tourist Trophy Race at Ulster.

Bathurst in 1939, John Sherwood (18) and John Barraclough (17) line up side by side in their NE Magnettes. Sherwood had imported both cars and promptly sold NA 0520 (no. 17) to Barraclough. The latter also later owned NA 0516 (no. 18) in post–war years.

John Barraclough wheels his NE Magnette down through The Esses at Bathurst in 1939.

On his way to victory in the 150–Mile race at Bathurst in 1939 is John Sherwood in his MG NE Magnette.

L. Boyle in an N–type MG Magnette, number 22, at Bathurst, Easter 1939.

Colin Dunne's ex–Prince Bira MG K3 at the October 1939 Bathurst meeting. Dunne and his wife were killed in an accident in their BMW 328 between races at Phillip Island in 1940.

Tom Lancey raced this stripped MG TA at Bathurst in the Easter 1939 meeting.

Yet another stripped MG TA, this one is John Nind's, at Bathurst for the October 1939 meeting.

J. B. Suttor also raced a stripped MG TA at Bathurst in October 1939, the T–series rapidly becoming a mainstay in Australian racing.

Hope Bartlett gives a passenger a thrill as he plunges down through The Esses at Bathurst in 1939 with his supercharged MG Q–type. Note the huge crowd, natural grandstand, and total lack of any kind of fencing.

Alan Tomlinson from West Australia, the youngest ever winner of the Australian Grand Prix, flashes over the finish line at Lobethal in South Australia in 1939 with his racing–bodied MG TA special.

Above: John Barraclough driving the 'NA 0520' MG NE Magnette in sports car trim, with mudguards and lights attached, at Penrith Speedway in 1938.

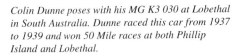

Colin Dunne poses with his MG K3 030 at Lobethal in South Australia. Dunne raced this car from 1937 to 1939 and won 50 Mile races at both Phillip Island and Lobethal.

Colin Dunne in action at Lobethal in 1939 with his supercharged MG K3. Of around 33 MG K3s built, an amazing seven examples now reside in Australia.

Above: John Barraclough posing with his road car, an MG SA saloon, known as the '2–litre' although the engine was in fact a 2.3–litre six cylinder. These cars were built from 1936 to 1939 and 28 of them remain on the MG Pre–War Register of Australia at the time of writing.

A handsome and refined derivative of the six–cylinder SA — called WA — was produced in 1938 with a 2.6–litre engine. World War Two intervened and only 370 were built.

FOR SALE

One of Australia's Most Successful Racing Cars

N.E. TYPE ULSTER M.G. MAGNETTE.

The above car is a works model N.E. type Ulster Magnette; there were only 14 of these cars ever produced by the factory, being specially built to compete in English and Continental sports' car races. This particular car was held in reserve by the M.G. team and was unused at the end of the season.

This N.E. type after leaving the factory was specially modified by R. R. Jackson, of Brooklands, who had an ENV close ratio gearbox fitted, special brakes, glacier metal bearings and a host of extras. All these improvements can be verified by the original correspondence which can be produced.

The car was imported to this country by Mr. J. O. Sherwood, who, among other events, won the 150 mile Bathurst Road Race in 1939. The certified speeds of this vehicle include a Brooklands' lap speed of 102.3 miles per hour as well as a standing lap speed of 86 miles per hour.

The N.E. type is the ideal vehicle for an enthusiast who requires a racing car combined with an ultra fast every day touring car, and is undoubtedly one of the prettiest sports cars on the road and will be sold with complete touring equipment. For definite sale at pegged price of £805, if necessary will accept other vehicle in part exchange.

For further information: Curry Engineering Works, 57 Malvern Road, East Prahran, Victoria. Windsor 1659.

This page: No model made a greater contribution to MG's fame than the TC, produced from 1945 to 1949. The first MG to reach volume production status (10,000 in four years), it became Britain's first postwar export success. Just over 2000 were shipped to the USA, where it was a cult car, and the two-seater also sold strongly in Australia. The TC design was derived from the 1939 TB which, in turn, was a development of the 1936 TA. Although dated when it appeared, the 1.25-litre TC proved enormously popular and very successful in a variety of motor sports.

THE 1946 M.G. T.C. MODEL

Just released by the Australian agents is the new version of the popular M.G. Midget series, known as the T.C. This model is similar to the T.B. that was produced just prior to the war. There were a few of these models sold in this country before the commencement of hostilities. The new T.C. is an open two-seater of typical Midget style—the established price is understood to be £594/10/- plus sales tax (Melbourne).

MOTOR FEATURES.

The engine is similar to the earlier " T " series, having 4-cylinders with the cylinder block and crankcase cast as one unit. The detachable head carries the overhead valves which are operated by push-rods.

The exceptionally rigid counterbalanced crankshaft is carried in three bearings. The connecting rods are provided with thin-wall stell-backed bearings, which ensure long life and can be quickly renewed if necessary.

Light alloy Aerolite pistons are employed, there being two compression and one slotted oil rings.

The inlet valves are slightly larger than the exhaust valves, and the mixture is provided by means of a two semi-downdraft S.U. carburettors. They are provided with a manual mixture control. Each carburettor is mounted on a light-alloy manifold, a single air silencer and cleaner supplies the air to both carburettors.

The oil is fed to all bearings by means of a large-capacity pump, through an oil filter at a pressure of between 40 lb. and 50 lb.

A float-on oil pick-up ensures that only clean oil is fed to the pump. The large ribbed alloy sump contains over a gallon of oil. The camshaft is driven by a duplex chain, and is mounted

SPECIFICATIONS OF T.C. M.G. MIDGET.	
Cubic Capacity	1,250 c.c.
Cylinders	4
Bore	66.5 m.m.
Stroke	90 m.m.
Comp. Ratio	7½ to 1
Valve Position	Push rod O.H.V.
Max. Power	54.4 B.H.P. at 5,200 r.p.m.
Ignition	12 volt Coil
Fuel Pump	S.U. electric
Electrical System	Lucas 12 Volt
First Gear	17.32 to 1
Second Gear	10 to 1
Third Gear	6.93 to 1
Fourth Gear	5.125 to 1
Reverse	17.32 to 1
Brakes	Lockheed Hydraulic
Drums	9 x 1½ inches
Wheelbase	7 ft. 10 in.
Track, front	3 ft. 9 in.
Track, rear	3 ft. 9 in.
Weight	15½ cwt.
Wheels	19 in.

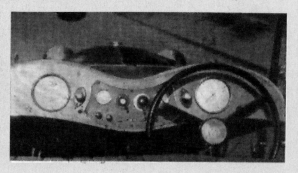

fairly high in the motor, so reducing the length of the push-rods; all valves are controlled by double valve springs.

SYNCHROMESH ON THREE GEARS.

The power from the motor is transmitted to the gearbox by means of a single plate Borg and Beck clutch. The flywheel is lighter than the earlier T.A. models, and with synchromesh on the three high ratios, it is possible to make very slick gear changes without double clutching. The gearbox is provided with a remote-control gear lever. Top gear gives 20 m.p.h. at 1,260 r.p.m.

CHASSIS FEATURES.

The chassis is the channel-section type, with the chassis passing under the rear axle. The half-elliptic, flat rear springs are mounted outside the chassis to prevent body roll when cornering.

The Lockheed hydraulic brakes have 9 in. cast iron drums with deep stiffening ribs which also assists heat dissipation. The brakes can be applied hard, with no sign of fading out. The hand brake is of the racing "fly off" type.

BODY.

Although similar to the earlier "T" series in appearance, the body of the T.C. is 4 ins. wider at the seating position, with a marked improvement to comfort, particularly when the side curtains are in position.

The latter components are provided with very stiff frames and when the hood is raised the car has all the comforts of a coupe, and still retains its good appearance. In the luggage compartment is a special locker for the stowing of the side curtains when not in use.

With usual M.G. practice, the 13-gallon tank is placed externally at the rear of the body, has a quick-release filler cap, and a self-warning 2-gallon reserve.

The instrument panel has a large Jaeger rev-counter and speedometer and all other necessary instruments.

The steering wheel is a Bluemel, spring spokes; the windscreen will fold forward and the windscreen wipers are the electric type.

GENERAL.

With 55 B.H.P., which gives a power to weight ratio of nearly 70 B.H.P. per ton, the performance of this car should be exceptional. It is reasonable to suppose that the T.C. is capable of crusing at 65 to 70 miles on our open roads, without over stressing the motor.

The coachwork is of the traditional English craftsmanship, and high quality trim and fittings are evident.

With their very strong chassis frames and unburstable engines, TCs and subsequent TDs were used as the basis of numerous road/race specials. The stylish Sydney–made Buchanan (produced from 1956 to 1958) was a prime example. It proved it could 'go' as well as 'show' when one won the Queensland Hillclimb Championship. More than 80 were made.

Action aplenty at the Mt Druitt track near Sydney in early 1949. Stuart Todhunter (MG J2) narrowly avoids a self–destructing special.

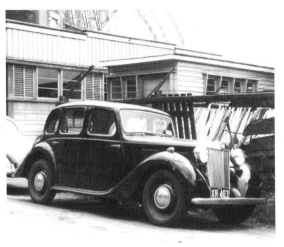

While the TC was in production, Abingdon decided to update a compact four–door sedan that had been designed before the war in prototype form. The Y–type had a single–carburettor version of the TC's 1.25–litre engine but a more up–to–date chassis with independent front suspension and rack–and–pinion steering. (The chassis was largely the work of Alex Issigonis, of Mini Minor fame and was subsequently shortened as the basis of the TD two–seater). The Y–type sedan was judged to be comfortable but a little too heavy for its engine size and many owners had it reworked for extra power. In late 1948, the Y–type sedan was joined by a four–seater tourer, with two carburettors and a lighter body. Compared with the TC, the tourer looked ponderous and, not surprisingly, sold poorly. It was withdrawn after only 877 had been made. In contrast, nearly 7500 sedans were made.

Above: Alf Najar (21) in his special–bodied MG TB and John Nind (22) in a more standard, but stripped, MG TB, line up for the start at Bathurst in October 1946. Behind them is the special–bodied MG TA of Bill McLachlan.

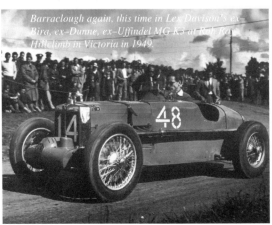

Barraclough again, this time in Lex Davison's ex–Bira, ex–Dunne, ex–Uffindel MG K3 at Rob Roy Hillclimb in Victoria in 1949.

John Barraclough at the wheel of Bill Nunn's MG TB with standard bodywork at Bathurst in 1946.

Seen here with Mazda MX5s — the car some say is its spiritual successor — the TD was an evolution of the TC, using the Y-type's superior chassis. It offered improved performance, more riding comfort and better handling than the TC. Produced from 1949 to 1953 in TD and TD2 forms, it outsold the TC by three-to-one in the US.

a new **MG** midget

THE SERIES "T.D."

It's here, the latest addition to the M.G. line of thoroughbreds . . . maintaining all those exceptional qualities of speed, manoeuvrability and ease of handling that have made M.G. midgets famous the world over as the enthusiasts car . . . bringing further advances in design and comfort that make this new model decidedly modern, yet still very definitely "M.G.". It's wider, roomier, better looking and with independent front suspension and rack and pinion steering, better riding and even more roadworthy than its famous predecessor. Yes, more than ever, it's M.G. for motoring at its exhilarating best!

Grand new features that make this the finest Midget ever

★ Coil sprung independent front wheel suspension.

★ Direct acting rack and pinion steering.

★ Hypoid rear axle.

★ New disc-type wheels with 5.50 x 15 tyres.

★ Increased luggage space.

★ New facia with separate speedometer and rev. counter.

★ Twin wind-tone horns.

★ Bumpers and over-riders.

★ 4" wider, 5" longer body than before.

Maintaining the Breed . .

Sole Distributors for Victoria and Southern Riverina.

LANE'S MOTORS PTY. LTD.

89-109 EXHIBITION ST., MELBOURNE - PHONE: CENT. 10490

The Easter Bathurst races in 1948 were something of an MG benefit. Here Curly Brydon heads a cluster of MGs out of the first corner in the 100 Mile Handicap.

Rita and Charles Rubin made one of the most extraordinary MG trips ever after deciding to celebrate their marriage by driving from Sydney to London. The red 1950 TD already had more than 80,000km on the clock but, in 1957, they shipped it to Bombay and commenced the 16,000km drive to Europe. Undeterred by the limited luggage space and unavailability of service back–up, they tackled some of the worst roads imaginable. They suffered several broken springs and a seized brake master cylinder but, with makeshift repairs and after 41 days of driving, they reached London with the car largely intact. They had averaged a daily distance of 384km.

The new series TD M.G. Midget bears a strong outward resemblance to its predecessors, except for the disc wheels, but is wider and more roomy; it retains the well-tried 1,250 c.c. pushrod engine, in a completely new chassis with greatly improved suspension and steering.

THE M.G. MIDGET SERIES TD

Chassis Redesigned—I.F.S., Rack and Pinion Steering

So far as appearance is concerned, the new Series TD M.G. has enough in common with the Series TC, which it supplants, to leave no doubt that it is the latest example of a long line of M.G. Midgets, cars which are known wherever there is sporting motoring. The most apparent outward change is the substitution of bolt-on pressed steel discs for centrelock wire wheels, the manufacturers giving as their reason for this substitution that it is necessary because of design considerations to do with the independent front suspension.

Otherwise, the mixture is largely as before; the body is wider across the seat and has more room for luggage, bumper bars with over-riders are fitted front and rear, and the front mudguards have been subtly altered in shape. Apart from dimensional modifications to fit in with the body, the hood and sidecurtains are unaltered, and should maintain the fine reputation for all-weather snugness which the TC earned; the dashboard instruments have been regrouped to allow space for a glovebox in front of the passenger, and a lower propeller shaft hump makes it easier to carry three passengers abreast. The distinctive M.G. radiator shell and separate headlamps are retained.

Mechanically, there have been several changes, but these have been confined mainly to chassis design. This has very little in common with that of the TC, as it has independent front suspension, steering by rack and pinion, and box section side-members which pass over instead of under the rear axle. Semi-elliptic springs are retained to suspend the back axle, which has hypoid bevel gears; gearbox ratios are wider and, though the wheels are smaller, the final drive ratio remains the same, as the TD is appreciably heavier than the TC.

Engine Unchanged.

Though earlier rumours had it that the TD would use a modified and tuned version of the overhead camshaft 4/50 Wolseley engine, on the face of it a most suitable power unit, the well known and well tried four cylinder pushrod engine common to the Series TB and TC cars is

retained. Though most M.G. enthusiasts are familiar with the characteristics of this motor, we feel that a brief recapitulation of its main features will not go amiss.

With four cylinders of 66.5 x 90 m.m. bore and stroke, capacity is 1,250 c.c., and, on a compression ratio of 7.25 to 1, 54.4 b.h.p. are realised at 5,200 r.p.m. A booklet published by the Nuffield organisation gives full details of various expedients whereby increased power can be obtained, the ultimate development recommended, consistent with reliability, involving the use of a Shorrock supercharger, and resulting in close to 100 b.h.p. being available. The willingness to work of the TC engine being well known, there is a lot to be said for the decision to fit it to the TD in place of the new overhead camshaft unit.

M.G. SERIES TD SPECIFICATIONS	
Engine	4-cylinder.
Bore and Stroke	66.5 x 90 m.m.
Capacity	1,250 c.c.
Valves	O.H. pushrod.
Compression ratio	7.25 to 1.
Maximum power	54.4 b.h.p. at 5,200 r.p.m.
Carburettors	Twin S.U. semi-downdraught.
Fuel pump	S.U. electric.
Ignition	Coil and automatic advance distributor.
Electrical System	12V. CVC, 51 amp./hr. capacity.
Cooling	Pump and fan with thermostat.
Lubrication	Pressure, 9 pint sump.
Oil filter	Full-flow.
Clutch	Single dry plate Borg and Beck.
Gearbox	4-speed, synch. 2, 3 and 4, cent. rem. control.
Gear ratios—1st	17.938 to 1.
2nd	10.609 to 1.
3rd	7.098 to 1.
Top	5.125 to 1.
Optional back axle ratio	4.55 to 1.
Propeller shaft	Open Hardy-Spicer.
Final drive	Hypoid bevel.
Steering gear	Rack and pinion.
Suspension (front)	Independent coil and wishbone.
(rear)	Semi-elliptic.
Shock absorbers	Luvax-Girling hydraulic.
Brakes	Lockheed hydraulic (2LS front).
Brake drum diameter	9 in.
Friction lining area	99.5 sq. in.
Wheelbase	7 ft. 10 in.
Track (front)	3 ft; 11¾ in.
(rear)	4 ft. 2 in.
Length overall	12 ft. 1 in.
Width overall	4 ft. 10¾ in.
Height overall (hood up)	4 ft. 5 in.
Ground clearance	6 in.
Tyres	5.50 x 15 ELP.
Wheels	Bolt-on pressed steel discs.
Weight	17 cwt. 2 qr.

Two valves per cylinder, with dual valve springs, are opened by forged rocker arms, operated by tubular push-rods and chill cast iron tappets from the chain driven camshaft. Lubrication is force feed throughout, from a large capacity gear type oil pump in the nine pint aluminium alloy sump; a full-flow oil filter is fitted. On the right hand side of the head, two semi-downdraught SU carburettors draw air through a new design of oil bath filter; they are mounted on a cast aluminium manifold which incorporates a large bore balance pipe, and feed two siamised inlet ports apiece. On the same side, four separate exhaust ports have a fan shaped cast iron manifold through which they exhaust into a single tail pipe and absorption type silencer.

Speedometer and rev counter are now grouped in front of the driver, leaving room on the left hand side of the dash for a capacious glovebox, in which a radio set can be fitted if desired. The new steering wheel is adjustable for column length.

Substantial bumper bars have over-riders, front and rear; there is a different spare wheel mounting, which can be supplied modified to carry two spares. Tail lights are set in the back mudguards.

Pump and fan cooling is thermostatically controlled; a single SU electric pump feeds the carburettors from the 11-gallon rear tank, which is fitted with a quick release filler cap and has the familiar flashing light warning signal when fuel level is low. The Lucas distributor has automatic advance, is mounted on the left hand side of the engine, and driven by right angle helical gears from the camshaft, firing one 14 m.m. plug per cylinder. Aerolite aluminium alloy pistons have two compression rings and one oil scraper each; the gudgeon pins are clamped in the little ends of the forged steel, I-section connecting rods. All crankshaft bearings are of the thin walled, steel backed variety, with white metal bearing surfaces. The crankshaft has three main bearings; it is counterbalanced, and drives the camshaft by silent chain at its front end. A vee-belt drives the dynamo and rev counter, the water pump, and the fan.

A single plate Borg and Beck clutch transmits the power to an excellent four-speed synchromesh gearbox, with ratio selection governed, as before, by a short lever through a remote control mechanism integral with the gearbox top; a dipstick is provided so that oil level can be checked easily. Gear ratios are more widely spaced than those of the TC, being 5.125, 7.098, 10.609 and 17.938 to 1.

Chassis Changes

Electrically welded throughout, the chassis frame is a completely new design. It has substantial box section side members, which have a pronounced kick up at the rear to pass above the back axle; these are joined in front by a box section cross member, elsewhere by tubular cross members, and there is a tubular arch member under the scuttle which supports the steering column. The independent front suspension has upper and lower wishbones of unequal length; rubber bushings are used at all pivot points in the suspension except the inner ends of the upper control arms, which swing on Luvax-Girling double-acting hydraulic shock absorbers. Coil springs are the suspension media, with rubber buffers to limit wheel movement both in bump and in rebound. The steering swivel pins have buttress threaded bearings.

Steering is of the helical rack and pinion type, carried in front of the wheel centre line; the ends of the rack are shrouded by synthetic rubber bellows, and are joined to the wheel steering arms by ball-jointed tie-rods. The steering column, fitted with a flexible joint near its lower end, carries a three spoke spring wheel which has a three inch adjustment. 2¾ turns take the steering from lock to lock,

turning circle being 31 feet right and left hand.

The back axle is suspended on semi-elliptic leaf springs, each of seven plates with rubber interlays; the shackles have rubber bushings. Luvax-Girling double-acting hydraulic shock absorbers are fitted, as in front. The axle is of the semi-floating type, and has hypoid bevel final drive gears, with a ratio of 5.125 to 1—as in the TC—and a Hardy-Spicer propeller shaft.

Brakes, although they have the same drum diameter as those of the TC, now have two leading shoes in front; there is slightly less friction lining area, but this should be offset by the greater efficiency. The hand-brake retains its racing type fly-off ratchet lever, but this has been moved to lie horizontally between the seats. It takes effect on the back wheels through a cable linkage. 15 inch disc wheels carry 5.50 x 15 tyres—6.00 by 15 wheels and tyres can be supplied for competition work—and the smaller effective wheel diameter gives a speed in top gear of 14.42 m.p.h. per 1,000 r.p.m. as against the 15.84 m.p.h. per 1,000 r.p.m. of the TC. This has the effect of dropping road speed in top gear at an average piston speed of 2,500 f.p.m. from 66.4 m.p.h. to 61.2 m.p.h., but an alternate pair of bevels of 4.55 to 1 ratio can be supplied to order, using which, equivalent figures are 16.25 m.p.h.—1,000 r.p.m., and 69 m.p.h. at 2,500 f.p.m. piston speed.

Body Alterations.

While the general outline of the TC has been preserved, the TD body has been redesigned to make it four inches wider, its width at elbow level being 45 inches. This widening process has extended to the luggage compartment behind the seat squab, which is appreciably more commodious. By using hypoid bevel final drive, it has been possible to dispense with a good deal of the central hump of the TC, so that three passengers can be accommodated abreast with considerably less discomfort than before. Seat cushions are separate, with the handbrake lever lying between them; they slide backwards and forwards for adjustment, and squab rake can be adjusted. High grade leather trim is used throughout.

Covered in leathercloth to match the trim, the dashboard has been rearranged so that the separate, 5 inch diameter, speedometer and rev counter (which embodies an electric clock) are set side by side in front of the driver; the oil pressure gauge, ammeter, ignition switch, combination horn button and dip switch, and minor engine controls, are grouped in a central panel. The left hand side of the dash board now has a roomy glovebox with locking lid, in which a radio set can be fitted if required. A twin-arm Lucas screenwiper is fitted to the fold-flat windscreen, and the driving mirror is set between the scuttle humps.

Twin wind-tone horns, with soft and loud tone control, are carried under the bonnet, as are the toolbox and battery. The spare wheel is carried on a tubular mounting behind the sloping rear tank, and a rear light is sunk into each back mudguard. Extra equipment available includes a dual spare wheel mounting, 6.00 x 16 rear wheels and tyres for competitions, a special chromium plated luggage grid, chromium plated badge bar and foglight mounting, and the higher back axle ratio.

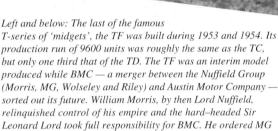

Doug Chivas — later a leading Australian touring car driver — getting the most out of a TD in 1953.

Left and below: The last of the famous T-series of 'midgets', the TF was built during 1953 and 1954. Its production run of 9600 units was roughly the same as the TC, but only one third that of the TD. The TF was an interim model produced while BMC — a merger between the Nuffield Group (Morris, MG, Wolseley and Riley) and Austin Motor Company — sorted out its future. William Morris, by then Lord Nuffield, relinquished control of his empire and the hard–headed Sir Leonard Lord took full responsibility for BMC. He ordered MG to cancel plans to replace the TD with an 'aero' shape, conceived in 1951 and tested in prototype form at Le Mans. Mr Lord did not want MG to compete with the Austin–Healey due in late 1952. In despair, MG management facelifted the TD by flaring the headlamps into the guards and fitting a sloping radiator grille. The cockpit was revamped with bucket seats and a more attractive instrument panel. The British press greeted the TF with faint praise but America's noted auto writer, Tom McGill, described it as 'Mrs Casey's dead cat slightly warmed over'. Even when a 1.5–litre engine was fitted during the production run, sales lagged behind the competition. However history has been far kinder to the TF, with some collectors calling it the most desirable of the T–series.

The new M.G. TF is a small sports car with big performance, and with excellent handling qualities is the best M.G. so far produced.

THE M.G. SERIES TF

Further Detail Development Around the XPAG Engine

M.G. TF SPECIFICATIONS

Engine	4-cylinder
Dimensions	66.5 x 90 m.m., 1,250 c.c.
Valves	O.H. pushrod
Compression ratio	8 to 1
Maximum b.h.p.	57.5 at 5,500 r.p.m.
Carburettors	2 S.U. semi-downdraught
Fuel feed	S.U. electric pump
Ignition	Coil and distributor
Electrical system	12V., 51 amp./hr.
Oil filter	Full flow
Clutch	8 in. Borg and Beck
Gearbox	4-speed, synch. 2, 3 and 4, central lever.
Gear ratios: 1st	17.06
2nd	10.09
3rd	6.725
Top	4.875
Propeller shaft	Open Hardy-Spicer
Final drive	Hypoid bevel
Steering gear	Rack and pinion
Suspension (front)	Ind. coil & wishbones
(rear)	Semi-elliptic leaf
Shock absorbers	Armstrong
Brakes	Lockheed Hydraulic, 2LS front
Brake drum diameter	9 in.
Friction lining area	99.5 sq. in.
Wheelbase	7 ft. 10 in.
Track (front)	4 ft. 0½ in.
(rear)	4 ft. 2 in.
Length overall	12 ft. 3 in.
Width overall	4 ft. 11½ in.
Height overall	4 ft. 4½ in.
Ground clearance	6 in.
Turning circle	31 ft.
Tyres	5.50 x 15, centrelock wire wheels
Weight (approximate)	17½ cwt.

Amongst the most long-suffering and abused motors in the history of automobile engineering must be counted the series XPAG engine as fitted to the series TB, TC, TD, and now TF M.G.'s—also, in slightly modified form, to the Y series saloon and tourer, and to the 4/44 Wolseley of recent date. On appearances, there is precious little to recommend this engine, a very conventional push-rod o.h.v. four cylinder stemming originally from its cousin, the Morris 10/4, but for sheer guts and capacity to take punishment for long periods without serious diminution of output, the XPAG compels our respect. If given proper maintenance it works sweetly for many thousands of miles; admittedly it has its quirks,

such as necessity for frequent valve clearance adjustment, a tendency to go through cam followers and timing chains, and that quite inexplicable feature of design the connecting rod little end pinch bolt, but these shortcomings are outweighed in the eyes of the modern M.G. enthusiast by its many sterling characteristics. There are some, of course, who deny that it is an M.G. at all, holding firmly to the opinion that the last of the breed was the PB; but who knows what trends would have been seen had the late and revered Cecil Kimber survived and been given a free hand?

Latest open car of the line is the new series TF, now to be seen around in increasing numbers; as has been the custom over the years, there are few really radical differences, the tendency being more towards detail development and change. Body lines, though recognisable, are altered, for the better in this contributor's opinion; the seats are more comfortable, and wholesale adoption of wire centrelock is a very welcome return of an endearing M.G. feature. On the debit side, the new bonnet arrangements make the engine less accessible.

We observe with little pleasure, also, that the M.G. has now, in common with certain other cars bearing once noble names, a dummy radiator cap crowning its traditional shell.

Slightly Souped XPAG

For the most part, the TF engine is the same as before, except for detail modifications which have improved power at the top end of the scale, but not so much at

ordinary traffic speeds. It has overhead valves, slightly inclined, in line fore and aft, operated by rockers and pushrods from the later type camshaft with improved quietening ramps on the cams; the compression ratio has been raised from 7¼ to 8 to 1, with questionable benefit to Australian users until fuel of reasonable octane rating is generally available.

From 1¼ inch S.U. carburettors to larger inlet valves, the induction tract has been enlarged right through, with benefit to breathing; exhaust valves are the same size and so is the exhaust system as far as the silencer, but a larger diameter tail pipe will reduce back pressure and lessen any tendency towards running-on, noticeable in earlier models. Stronger valve springs have raised the incidence of valve crash to 6,000 r.p.m.; the nett result of these modifications has been to increase maximum b.h.p. by around 7 per cent., which is naturally reflected in road performance.

Stroke-bore ratio is 1.35 to 1, a limiting factor when really serious hotting-up is contemplated but, in our mind, favourable to reasonably long engine life; the crankshaft runs in three slipper type main bearings, with slipper bearings for con rods, and an oversize oil pump provides copious lubrication under all but the most arduous conditions.

The clutch is an 8 inch diameter Borg and Beck single dry plate; gearbox ratios have been slightly altered towards the more pleasant ones which were characteristic of the TC, and the synchromesh arrangements are improved. Final

With cleaned up body lines, more streamlining and wire wheels, the appearance is pleasant from all angles.

drive ratio is now 4.875 as against 5.125, giving approximately a 5 per cent. increase in m.p.h. per 1,000 r.p.m., and obviating for us personally most of the unconscious urge to go on changing up after top is engaged, as we do in a TD. As against this, the larger carburettors and higher ratio combine to reduce ever so slightly but noticeably the top gear acceleration at speeds of around 30 m.p.h.

Suspension and chassis frame are similar to those of the TD, with detail improvements; the rack and pinion steering has slightly more damping which reduces road shock at the wheel without detracting from sensitivity, and the really good steering lock is unchanged. Brakes are the same size but better cooled with the wire wheels and so more likely to perform with consistent reliability. As before, the handbrake lever lies horizontally between the seats, and has a fly-off ratchet action, calculated to bemuse any parking station attendant who hasn't encountered one previously. Shock absorbers are double acting piston type Armstrong, and seem to be of adequate size for their job, riding being firm but quite comfortable and road holding excellent.

Besides the knock-off wire wheels, which are only right and proper on a sports car (we could never quite stomach those excuses about front-end geometry and steering tie-rod ends which were offered as apologia for the tin disc wheels

of the TD) about the greatest single improvement lies in the seating accommodation. Seats are individual, very well shaped for lateral support and most comfortable to sit in, also individually adjustable for reach, so that by using the steering wheel adjustment it is possible readily to arrive at an almost perfect driving position.

Finish, inside and out, is good; the leather covered sponge rubber crash pad across the scuttle looks cute but may not stand up to weathering; a new material for hood and tonneau cover is very good indeed. Side curtains live in a box under the floor of the tonneau, lying flat; although this reduces luggage space to a certain extent, it does away with the complicated drill essential to fitting the TD curtains into their little box against the fuel tank.

Problems of production are the main gainers from the new dashboard, adaptable equally to right or left hand drive; octagonal instruments are recessed into a

central panel, very reminiscent of the Y-type, and minor control knobs are arranged below them, set at an awkward angle. The panel is flanked by two open fronted compartments, with a grab rail above on the passenger's side. From personal preference we regret the passing of the TC panel, which was handsome and functional, and had room for the addition of essential instruments, as did that of the TD to a lesser extent. The central driving mirror is well placed but allowances must be made for the blind spot it creates; its substantial mounting does away with irritating vibration.

Push buttons release the bonnet top catches; fixed side panels cut down accessibility to carburettors, distributor and oil filter to some extent, but can be removed with some trouble after undoing a number of screws which hold them in place. A heavy duty screenwiper motor is mounted on the engine side of the bulkhead, operating the wiper arms by remote control.

Summing up, we think the TF's good points achieve balance with such features as are personally less desirable, and expect that it will enjoy equal popularity amongst enthusiasts with all M.G.'s that have gone before it.

The easily read instruments are grouped in the centre of the dash with handy gloveboxes on either side. The steering column is adjustable for length.

AUSTRALIAN MOTOR SPORTS, September, 1954

A. Maxwell at Altona (Victoria) in mid–1954, making what was claimed to be the TF's first competition appearance in Australia.

Below: All T–series cars had chassis dynamics which out–performed the relatively small engines, so non–standard transplants became common for competition work. Here Sydney's Holt Binnie has his Holden–engined TF in full flight.

The REDeX Round Australia Trials of the 1950s created enormous public interest. As with virtually all other motor sport events in this era, the MG brand was represented. This is the TD that Don Bain and Les Slaughter campaigned strongly in the 1954 event. Unfortunately, Slaughter campaigned a TF with Bill Mayes in the Ampol Trial two years later with tragic results. While running in third place towards the finish of the event, the pair rolled the car into a creek and both were drowned..

Fishermans Bend airstrip, 1956. Laurie Viney (TF) has a slight altercation with the Austin 7 special of Don Dunoon.

The TF of R. Rothwell battles with a Zephyr convertible in a production car race at the Berkshire Park Airstrip (NSW).

MG by three! Typically frantic racing at Orange circuit (NSW) in 1955 or 1956. Peter Topen's MG TF leads the group.

The MG Special of Curly Brydon leads two other MG Specials driven by Col James and Ray Fowler in the Easter 1955 Bathurst meeting.

Facing pages:The decision to delay the introduction of a modern replacement for the TD proved disastrous and sales fell sharply. Finally BMC's management relented and a design office was re–established at Abingdon. The new engineering team — headed by Syd Enever — worked feverishly during 1955 to prepare the all–new A–type. The first production MG with an aerodynamic shape, it was similar in appearance to an earlier racing TD and based on the cars which had performed creditably at the 1955 Le Mans 24–hour race. Powered by a 1.5–litre BMC engine and endowed with the best roadholding of any MG sports car so far, the MGA was an immediate success. Over 100,000 were sold during a seven–year production run.

SOMETHING
DREAMS
ARE MADE OF.
THE NEW

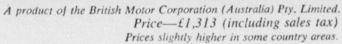

MARK II

*Left: Advertisement run in March 1955 issue of
Modern Motor.*

*The brilliant but flawed MGA Twin Cam engine
appeared in 1958, developed from the BMC B–series
unit, bored out to 1588ccs. It boosted power to 97bhp at
5000rpm. Just over 2000 MGA Twin Cams were built
during a two–year period. The engine proved a major
disappointment, needing frequent attention. It was easily
damaged by over–revving and, unless the fuel octane
rating, ignition timing and carburation settings were
exactly right, burned pistons and excessive oil consumption could result.*

*Below: The MGA Mk2 was launched in the UK in June
1961. This is a British car. Australian MGAs had wire
wheels; the 1600 MkI in 1960 had new tail–light clusters;
and the 1600 MkII, when released in Australia in 1962, had
horizontal tail–lights and recessed grille slats.*

While some fixed hard–top versions of the MGA were privately imported to Australia, local new car buyers wanting a closed sports car could buy only detachable hard–top versions like this one.

The 'A' was the first MG assembled in Australia. This photograph was taken in 1956 at the BMC plant at Zetland, NSW. Production of MGAs and MGBs continued there until 1972.

Sales always rose sharply when MG was able to established a new speed record. The company became a persistent and consistent record–breaker, with 42 international class records established during 30 years of active competition. The 1.5–litre Ex181 was built in 1957 and driven by Stirling Moss to 245.6mph (398km/h) on the Utah Salt Flats. Two years later, with the engine enlarged marginally, Phil Hill reached 254.9mph (413km/h) in the same car. This picture of Hill in action was the last time that the MG factory officially attempted to break a record.

Above: July 1961, Ralph Sach in Robin Orlando's MGA Twin–Cam leads Brian Foley's Austin Healey Sprite in the Australian GT Championship at Warwick Farm. Sach retired with loss of oil pressure. This car has been restored by Frank Hiscock in Cootamundra — probably the lowest mileage twin–cam in the world. Thirty–two years later, Michael Gunnell (right) proved that a 1959 MGA is still very fast during an historic meeting at Eastern Creek, NSW.

BMC employed badge engineering with great success during the 1950s, using the reputation of MG, Riley and Wolseley to lift the image of some very prosaic designs. However, the 1.5–litre ZA Magnette, produced from 1953 for six years in various forms, also added to MG's reputation with a series of competition successes. It also did well in the showroom, comfortably outselling the sportier TF.

Above: The cumbersome–looking Magnette Mk IV was much less successful than the ZA Magnette, selling less than half as many in the same period of time. With an extended wheelbase and heavier body than the ZA, it was powered by a fairly docile 1.6–litre 'four'. Available with an optional automatic transmission, its performance was decidedly less than MG enthusiasts expected.

Left: Another BMC exercise in badgemanship, the Midget was an MG version of the Austin–Healey Sprite Mk II. Mechanically, the two cars were the same but the Midget had some equipment advantages. Both were powered initially by 948cc A–series engines giving a top speed of 138km/h. The car pictured is a MkIII version with a 1275cc engine.

This page: The famous MGB (see caption overleaf).

This page and previous page: Just over 100,000 MGAs were built during a six–year run and, though there was much discussion about its replacement, no–one realised the company was about to produce its most successful model ever. Nor did they remotely suspect it could be virtually the last model to come from Abingdon. A total of 525,000 MGBs were built between 1962 and 1980 including GT V8s and the six–cylinder MGC. The MGB was the first MG sports car with a monocoque body. Although the design disappointed many diehards, it was without question superior to the MGA in virtually everything that mattered, including comfort, performance, handling and luggage space.

There is one car . . . every other sports car in the world tries to come up to . . . but can never quite make it . . . the "B" . . . the superlative MGB. This is the car with the magic ingredient that spells success. Its secret? A culmination of sporting achievements that go back to the very beginning of motor racing itself. The "B" — a living legend that goes to make up a great sports car. And now it's gone even further ahead... more sophisticated than ever with optional overdrive and automatic transmission. The "B". . . the superlative MGB . . . the car that separates the men from the boys. Why not see your BMC Dealer . . . and join the men who know the difference.

the car that has the
magic that spells success

MGB Mark II

MODERN MOTOR — JULY 1969

Australians were offered various after–market versions of the MGB hardtop. Car DZX 851, below, has a locally–made fibreglass top fitted by BMC Sportscar Centre, Sydney. Car EBT 776, left, has the all–steel factory coachwork, available only by private import from the UK.

The MGB was designed at a time when cars were subjected to far fewer safety regulations than now. Nevertheless, the extent of its resistance to rollover damage was unintentionally demonstrated when a large tree fell on a car parked in a Sydney suburb.

BMC Australia took great pride in assembling the MGB in its Sydney plant. This shot was taken on the second leg of the assembly line where the body shell, with most of the hardware fitted, was lowered onto the suspension units before moving on to receive the engine, transmission and driveshaft.

It was a proud day for Abingdon when George Turnbull watched the 250,000th MGB come off the line, accompanied by Old No 1. Mr Turnbull later left BMC/Leyland to help Hyundai establish a new plant in Korea.

*This page: Trapped by the trauma sweeping
through the parent company, BMC/Leyland, MG
made a low–budget attempt to revive its fortunes in
1967 with a six–cylinder version of the 'B'. Known as
MG 'C', it was powered by an existing BMC 3–litre
engine developing 180bhp. Overdrive or auto
transmission were optional. Some 9000 'Cs' were
built over two years.*

This page: The pictures tell it all. Executives at BMC Australia were so distressed when economic circumstances forced the closure of the MGB assembly line they organised a funeral and wake. MGs had been in local production for 16 years.

MG

M.G.B
BORN
4TH APR 1963
DIED
6TH NOV 1972
R.I.P

Powered by a 3.5–litre Rover engine, the MGB GT V8 made its debut in Britain in August 1973. It stayed in production for nearly four years but only 2600 were built.

By 1975,
the MGB was burdened with ugly
bumpers and a higher ride height (to raise the headlamp
height) to appease US legislators. By then a succession of managers at strife–torn
British Leyland were convinced that development money should be ploughed into Triumph, not MG. The
great marque was dying through lack of support from the head office bean–counters. Although Abingdon was to survive
another few years, there was already talk of closing it. Practically no development work had been done for five years even
though MG dealers around the world were demanding more modern cars.

Inevitably, some small–volume manufacturers used MG components in specialised bodywork. One of the better examples
was the Gilbern, one of the few cars ever made in Wales. This 1962 example with MGB mechanicals, including the 1.8–litre
engine, is thought to be the only Gilbern to come to Australia.

Also in Australia is this magnificent 1974 MG MGB GT V8, being raced by Sydney's Tony Hilton when in the UK.

Twelve years after the Abingdon factory ceased production of MGs, the Rover Group — the sole survivor of the original British Motor Corporation/Leyland fiasco — commenced limited production of the MG RV8. It is seen here with the 1962 MGB on which the new car is based.

modern
MOTOR

Registered at G.P.O., Sydney, for transmission as a periodical

**BETTER PETROL
FOR YOUR CAR**

PAGE 14

JUNE 1954

2'6

Distributed by
Consolidated Press

"**H**AMILTON continued at a speed which was greater than before, and during the next four laps he increased his average for the race by a full mile per hour. When he passed the grandstand, Crabtree was still clinging to the Magnette. He had been cornering his Midget with a daring that made the spectators gasp, so closely did he risk disaster —particularly on the turn into Ballaquayle Road, where again and again his machine pitched into a series of skids."

That is how Barre Lyndon describes a famous MG duel in his book "Circuit Dust"—a duel in the first Manin Beg race, through the streets of Douglas township on the Isle of Man, back in 1933.

The MG was already an institution then, and the years that followed added to its reputation, making it by far the most popular of all sports cars.

This year Australian motorists welcomed the latest addition to the legendary MG family—the TF model, which, like all its kin, is a direct descendant of the first MG, conceived and built in 1923 by Cecil Kimber, general manager of Morris Garages.

It's a big step from this original car—with its combination of a much-modified Hotchkiss engine, Morris Cowley radiator and parts and Kimber's genius—to the modern TF, designed and built entirely by the MG division of British Motors Corporation, and making quite a few concessions to modern ideas of stream-lining and appearance. But it's a safe bet that the TF will make a reputation for itself in the now well-established MG tradition.

There have been many well-designed sports cars, which have given excellent racing results; but none of them has ever been received with such overwhelming enthusiasm as the MG. In three short years, from when Kimber first persuaded W. R. Morris to build the MG, to 1926, when the terrific demand forced expansion to new premises, its name became synonymous with the keen motorist's ideal of an all-round sports car.

The year 1928 saw the appearance of the first MG Midget—true forerunner of today's TF. Basically constructed around the Morris Minor, it was the first real challenger to the Austin Seven, which until then had dominated the under 750 c.c. racing class.

The MG Story

Cecil Kimber persuaded his boss to build the first MG 31 years ago. It soon became the world's favorite sports car — and still is.

MODERN MOTOR — June 195

EVERY TRACK has its batch of MG's. Of ten starters in this Australian race, six belong to the breed. On the opposite page is the blown MG Special which Lieut.-Col. Goldie Gardner drove to smash several U.S. and world records in 1949. He clocked 159 m.p.h. for a flying mile.

In its touring body form this model was known as the M type. With its fabric body, 847 c.c. engine and developed power of 20 b.h.p., it soon pushed the Austin Seven — up to that time recognised as THE small sports car—into the background. Later the M type had a metal body fitted. Altogether over 3000 cars were produced in this form—a very substantial figure for those days.

Although several different MG types were produced between 1928 and 1935, most of them were made in limited numbers. Nevertheless, their design was so outstanding that the British name was at the head—or near the head—of trophy lists for racing and trials throughout the world.

Apart from the M type, these years saw the 14/40—first MG to be built in the firm's own factory; Mark IV, produced between 1927 and 1929—an improved 14/40, developing 35 b.h.p.; and Marks I, II, and III, built in the years 1930-32 (however, only about 1500 cars embracing these models were built altogether).

In the Midget class, following the M type, came the D type, built more as a touring car than for sporting work; the C type, a racing two-seater developing 37.4 b.h.p., with an 8.5/1 compression ratio. Although less than fifty were built of this model, many are still in service; they have proved extremely reliable and capable of 90 m.p.h.

The original M type was offered in touring form as the J1, and special supercharged racing models were designated J3 and J4.

Around these early years the successes gained by the MG's were highlighted when G. E. T. Eyston became the first man to exceed 100 m.p.h. in a 750 c.c. class car —an MG. Two years later, also in an MG, Eyston reached 120 m.p.h., and in the same year an MG won the Brooklands Racing Drivers' Club's 500-miler at an average speed of 96.29 m.p.h.

Although, in those years, the MG name became famous mainly through racing events, Kimber's brain-

ORIGINAL MG factory building shows signs of old age. Leaving it are two Y type export saloons. One car is labelled Malta, the other New York.

The first

CAREFULLY preserved to
this day, the first MG was
built in 1923. It had a
modified 11.9 h.p. Hotch
kiss engine with Morris
Cowley radiator and parts.
Designed as a fast sports
car, it was successful from
the start, and by 1926 the
factory was expanded to
meet the demand. The
first Midget wasn't built
till 1928.

The latest

TF series MG has chassis
of Mark II, originally produced for U.S. market.
Its 1250 c.c. push-rod
o.h.v. engine has com-
pression ratio raised from
$7\frac{1}{2}/1$ to 8/1. Twin carburettors and valves have
been enlarged; stronger
valve springs allow a safe
6000 r.p.m. Engine de-
velops $57\frac{1}{2}$ b.h.p. at 5500
r.p.m. Telescopic steer-
ing column, adjustable
seats, glove boxes give
added comfort.

child also earned itself a fine reputation as a touring
and trial car—and gave valiant service as the family
"buggy" as well.

The 1934-36 period saw the advent of the P types,
a total of 2525 being built under the model names PA
and PB. Some of these models reached Australia and still
have a good resale value here, being recognised as cars
capable of a good turn of speed, and at the same
time reliable for touring or family use.

The P type was a far more comfortable car than its
predecessors, and in the PB form, with the 939 c.c. engine, it overcame the serious opposition of the Le Mans
Singer, which had been challenging the MG records.
The PB was capable of 100 m.p.h. if supercharged, and
is still acclaimed by many devotees as the finest small
sports car ever built.

Next came the Q type, which featured the Wilson
pre-selector gearbox. Only one other MG—the K3—
was equipped with this famous unit.

Bigger Brothers

WHILE the name MG usually brings to mind the
small, simply designed sports car commonly seen
darting in and out of traffic like an overgrown motor-
cycle, during the 1930's the parent factory was also
building many successful larger models. The first of
the Magna models was the F1—a 6-cylinder tourer or
saloon, developing over 37 b.h.p.; this in turn was

followed by the F2 and F3, approximately 1300 of which
were built in the years 1931-33.

These models, together with the L types that followed
them, were also instrumental in helping to build the MG
family name. With a saloon model on the market, the
MG was no longer looked upon as purely a sporting
car, offering little comfort and not particularly suited
for the driver who wants to travel from A to B in the
greatest possible ease.

During the same period, in 1932, came the first
Magnette—the KA model, another 6-cylinder saloon.
Produced until 1936, the Magnette became a serious
opponent of the Maseratis, Sunbeams, Bentleys, Rileys
and Alfa-Romeos, which then dominated the racing and
trial field in the larger classes.

Such famous courses as the Mille Miglia, Italy;
Brooklands, England; Avus, Germany (or, to give it its
full title—**Avusrennen fur rennwagen**—Avus races for
racing chariots), and many others, all saw the big MG's
arrive and put up amazing performances. The MG's
were crowd-pleasers; they had spectacular drivers, and
the British were determined to win—and often did.

The Magnette's abilities were strikingly demonstrated
in 1933, when Tazio Nuvolari, recognised by many as
the world's best racing driver, decided to try out a K3.
He had never raced an English car before, and had never
even driven an MG; nor had he any previous experience
of the Wilson pre-selector gearbox, as fitted to this model.

MODERN MOTOR — June 1954

A few hours before the Royal Automobile Club's Ulster T. race was due to start, Nuvolari climbed into the 3, tried a slow lap, then did a couple of fast ones—and it was all. But he won the race, averaging a sizzling 6.6 m.p.h. for the 478-mile course and chalking up an erage of 81 m.p.h. for his best lap.

Nuvolari's performance got him a terrific ovation from e crowd, who appreciated the handicap of an un- miliar car. The race, regarded to this day as a classic, lped strengthen the reputation of both car and driver.

Only today are the twin sports of motor racing and otor trials coming back into favor, after the cline they suffered shortly before the war and during e war years. In the days of peak racing interest auto- obile and racing clubs took over whole areas and towns, nd the complete population would be out to see the vents. Perhaps today we have become a little **blasé** bout such events, but in the early '30's races and rac- ng cars—and especially the MG name—were regular ousehold bywords.

The first of the truly modern MG's appeared in 936; this was the TA model, a direct forerunner of he new TF, and more especially the TC, produced n far greater quantities than any other sports car as ever been.

The TA was little different in appearance from the well-known TC. It had a gearbox synchro-meshed in hird and top, Lockheed hydraulic brakes, and a 1292 c.c. engine developing 54.5 b.h.p. at 4000 r.p.m. The most surprising feature of the TA (in those days) was the push-rod engine — a change greeted by the enthusiasts with moans, groans, and forecasts of failure. However, as usual, the designers knew what they were doing — and the TA turned out to be a really astonishing little car. When tested on the Brooklands track in England, it lapped at an average of more than 90 m.p.h., which soon converted the unbelievers.

The TA, in its turn, was followed just before the war by the TB — a model with a slightly smaller

SIX-CYLINDER drophead saloon sold well in the 1930's. In photo below, Bill McLachlan's beetle-like TA Special (in four-wheel drift) is chased by Alf Najar's TB Special.

engine (1250 c.c., like the TF's). Despite this, it put up as good a performance as the TA, and has been raced with great success throughout the world.

One TB model in Australia was raced by Sydney driver Alf Najar eight years ago. As it performed so well in its original form, he decided to see what it could do when modified. With a new racing body and modified engine it repaid the owner's faith and hard work by winning the N.S.W. Grand Prix for him in October, 1946.

Postwar Brood

THE war, of course, brought a full stop to the development of the MG, and sporting enthusiasts had to wait till 1945, when the TC was produced.

The enthusiasts were not disappointed with the new MG "baby," and one of the most startling developments

was the enthusiasm the car aroused in the United States, which had never produced a good light sports car. TC's were exported in quantity to America, and soon MG clubs were springing up all over the country. (Today the bulk of MG's reserved for overseas trade goes straight to the U.S.A. to earn much-needed dollars for Britain.)

The TC received the same enthusiastic reception in Australia, soon becoming a common sight not only on the roads, but also on the tracks, where it quickly established a reputation of its own.

MG Magnette—a popular racer in Australia.

In Australia the TC's have won countless events at sports venues, including Bathurst, Nuriootpa, Point Cook, and other tracks throughout the country.

The quality of the MG was shown in 1949, when Lieut.-Colonel Goldie Gardner drove one to win new records in the under 750 c.c. class: the Flying Kilometre speed trial at an average speed of 159.198 m.p.h.; the Flying Mile at an average speed of 159.151 m.p.h.; and the Flying Five Kilometres at an average speed of 150.467 m.p.h.

Goldie Gardner used a blown MG TD engine for most of his speed record attempts. The Newcastle distributor for MG happened to be visiting England when this engine was being prepared. The engineers told him bench tests had shown that it should push the car along at 140 m.p.h. They were not far wrong: in the first speed attempt, before further modifications were carried out, Goldie Gardner reached just over 139 m.p.h. As the engine was never tried in a chassis in England, this demonstrates the rare ability of MG engineers to reconcile theory with practice.

Another famous postwar MG favorite is the Y type—a four-seat saloon with independent front suspension. The saloon was soon followed on the market by the Y type tourer, and both newcomers, somewhat different in design and style from the usual MG range, achieved popularity in a matter of months

The YA, first built in 1946, was an entirely new MG. It was produced until 1951, when it gave way to the modified YB, which continued until 1953. Australia is now waiting for the new Magnette, first to bear that name since the war. This will have a chassis-less body, fitted with a 1½-litre B.M.C. engine rated at 13.9 horse-power (R.A.C.) and developing 60 b.h.p. at 4600 r.p.m. Twin carburettors will further boost performance.

The Y-type engine, on the other hand, has gone into the new Wolseley 4/44. This engine first proved itself in Australia when Clive Cadden won the country's first saloon car race, at Mt. Druitt in 1950. Another of his successes was scored in the New South Wales hill-climb championship for saloons under 1500 c.c., held at King Edward Park, Newcastle, in 1952.

It may have been the excellent reception given the Y type that influenced the designers when they pro-

duced the TD, with its independent front-wheel suspension, smaller wheels, hub caps, and other refinements. The TD was not received with quite the same enthusiasm in Australia as previous models — the main objection being the smaller disk wheels, instead of knock-on wire wheels.

In the United States, on the other hand, the new features only served to heighten the MG's popularity; ownership of a "G" soon became "the thing" in society, and a necessity in sport. Proof of this is the fact that 30,000 MG's have been sold to U.S. enthusiasts since the war.

Latest Effort

NOW, as a result of more than 30 years' experience in building the world's most popular sports car, we have the brand-new TF.

The TF has two outstanding features that first meet the eye: headlights set into the mudguards, and knock-on wheels reintroduced to please Australian buyers. Disk-and-hubcap wheels are still fitted to models sold

A Q type MG that won many races for Frank Kleinig

elsewhere, but the sporty wire spokes have been specified as a "must" for Australian trade.

The reason behind our sportsmen's preference for knock-on wheels will be easily seen from the following incident:

During a recent race in New South Wales, an MG pulled into the pits with tyre trouble; eight seconds later it was on its way with a new wheel fitted.

While the chassis and general design of the TF are similar to those of the discontinued TD, the engine (developing 57½ b.h.p. at 5500 r.p.m.) is bigger and more powerful. With top revs at 6000, a top speed of 90 m.p.h. is possible from a TF in factory condition. What will happen when the experts get on the job, modifying the car for their own particular needs, is anyone's guess — but topping the 100 mark should prove a simple matter.

Generally the MG's body design has been improved by introducing the new inset headlights and providing a cleaner, more streamlined rear. It is a more comfortable car, too, with softer, individually adjustable seats, two glove boxes in the facia panel, and improved hood material

Is this new model as good a performer as its forebears? What are the details of its performance, pick-up and cornering? A road test will answer all these questions as soon as one of the TF's now in the country has run up the necessary mileage. But when you look back over the MG story and read the list of MG successes, it seems safe to predict that the TF will do all that the sportsmen expect of it—and perhaps a good deal more.

MODERN MOTOR — June 1954

THE TC series MG was first produced in England in November, 1945, and reached the Australian market in 1946. It superseded the TB model of 1939, but used the same 1250 c.c. overhead-valve engine.

Body changes rather than chassis changes characterise the differences between the TB and TC series; one easy means of distinguishing the models is the way the springs are coupled at the rear. On the TB they run in trunnions, whereas TC models use shackles.

Also, the chassis numbers start at 0251 and are prefixed TC. These numbers are stamped in two places: on a plate on the side of the gearbox and on the nearside chassis side member, just back of the front dumb-iron.

outer end of the pedal pivot pin, then pushing the pivot inwards through its bracket. Also, remove the accelerator pedal gear.

Undo the screws securing the ramp plate to the dash and lift the panel out. Remove the two leads from the starter motor terminal and the Bowden wire from the starter switch.

The gearbox top cover, complete with its remote control, can now be taken off (seats, carpets, rubber gearbox cover or gearbox carpet and floorboards having been removed previously).

It will be obvious that some of the components listed here will also need to be detached even if only the engine is to be withdrawn.

To break the transmission drive, uncouple the tailshaft at the rear of the gearbox. Always mark the

the radiator should be left loose until the position of the radiator core has been adjusted to suit the bonnet clearance.

The front engine mounting also acts as an engine stabiliser, and it is important not to compress the rubber too tightly, as otherwise excessive engine vibration may result.

To ensure correct assembly of this important mounting, first thread the bolt through the engine plate into the rubber mounting block and tighten in the normal way; then thread the small rubber block on to the bolt, with its small diameter inserted in the hole in the frame bracket. This is followed by a steel washer and a sleeve nut which is screwed up through the rubber block so that a slight tension is exerted on the rubber. While the sleeve nut is

KNOW YOUR MG TC

All TC engine numbers are prefixed XPAG; when the TD model was introduced in 1950, the letters TD were added to this designation and the prefix became XPAG/TD.

One peculiarity of the TC is the strange mixture of thread sizes used on it. The threads on nuts and bolts in the engine and gearbox are metric, yet those on the rest of the car are BSF—and the hexagon sizes of all nuts and bolt heads are Whitworth.

Engine Removal

The engine is generally taken out separately, leaving the gearbox in place; but if the floorboards are removed, the engine and gearbox can be drawn out as a complete assembly.

To remove the engine only, start by taking off the bonnet, then disconnect the radiator hoses, tie-rods and headlamp brackets from the shell. Take off the two nuts below the brackets and remove the radiator shell and core. Disconnect all pipes, wires and controls, then remove the steering gear complete.

Dismantle the front mounting assemblies and take the engine weight with slings fitted behind the front plate and below the flywheel housing. Remove the set-screws around the bell-housing, then draw the engine forward and lift out.

If the engine and gearbox are to come out as an assembly, the clutch operating chain must be disconnected from the pedal and the clutch and brake pedals removed. This is done by extracting the split-pin at the

two flanges before dismantling, to ensure that they are returned to their original position. If the drive is reassembled incorrectly, excessive vibration will result.

Remove all controls, petrol pipes and manifolds that would be detached if taking off the head, then remove speedo and rev-counter cables from the engine. Place a jack under the gearbox and take enough of the weight to allow the four main rear engine bolts (between gearbox and rubber mounting) to be removed. After taking the nuts and washers off the front engine bolts, unscrew the latter from the rubber mounting; the engine assembly can then be lifted clear.

When refitting the above parts, the securing nuts at the bottom of

held in this position, the lock-nut is fitted and fully tightened.

Pistons and Rods

To remove one or more conrods and pistons, drain the sump and raise the front of the car so that it can be placed on safety stands. After the engine oil has drained completely, remove the steering drag link, then unbolt and lower the sump to reach the big-end caps.

Always ensure that the engine parts are properly marked to ensure correct reassembly in their original positions.

After removing the split-pins and nuts from all the big-end bolts, the bottom caps can be withdrawn.

When separating a piston from its connecting rod, give special care to the pinch-bolt in the small end of

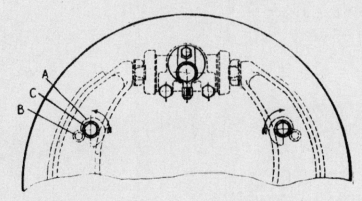

BRAKE shoe adjustment. See text for figure reference.

Seventieth of a series of articles on the care and maintenance of popular car models

the rod. This bolt fits into a groove in the gudgeon pin and must be taken right out. It is inadvisable to hold the rod in a vice while the pinch-bolt is undone, as the rod is likely to be damaged.

Special end pads (part No. T78) which are inserted into the open ends of the gudgeon and extend beyond the sides of the piston should be used (these allow the assembly to be gripped in a vice without fear of damage). But you can use two suitably sized bolts as a makeshift — provided they can be fitted so that they won't foul the piston in any way.

If it is necessary to replace or resize the pistons, the clearance between piston and cylinder wall should be .0015 to .0025in. This should be measured below the three top piston rings and at 90deg. to the gudgeon pin.

Three rings are used, two being compression rings and one slotted oil-control ring. When fitting new rings of either type, the gap (measured when they are compressed in the cylinder without the piston) should be .004 to .006in.

To ensure that the rings fit squarely in the bore, invert the piston and push down on the rings, checking each ring separately. Measure the gap at the top of the stroke, then push the ring to the bottom and re-check. Any difference between the two readings will indicate the amount of taper wear in the cylinder.

Never fit new rings in the top groove unless the lip or ridge in the cylinder has been honed out first — otherwise the ring lands may be damaged. Also, never use oversize pistons and rings to compensate for bore wear.

Finally, ensure that the ring gaps are evenly spaced around the pistons, with no two gaps opposite to each other, otherwise oil may travel up and combustion gases blow down and into the crankcase.

The conrods are fitted with thin, replaceable steel-backed white-metal bearing shells. These bearings cannot be taken up by adjustment and must be replaced if worn.

Camshaft Removal

To remove the camshaft, the tappets must first be withdrawn from their guides (after lifting the rocker cover and taking out the pushrods). Next take off the distributor and remove the oil pump. A locking screw is the only fitting holding the distributor in place, while the oil pump is released by removing the bolts securing it to the cylinder block.

Now remove the timing chain and sprockets — which, of course, means taking off the sump, crankshaft pulley and timing case. A special tool (part No. T123) is available to remove the pulley and sprockets, but any puller which will withdraw the sprockets without damaging them may be employed.

Draw the camshaft forward from its rear main bearing through the front bearing, carrying the centre bearing with it. The dowel screw which

TUNING DATA

Bore: 66.5mm.
Stroke: 90mm.
Capacity: 1250 c.c.
Compression ratio: 7.25/7.5 to 1.
Maximum b.h.p.: 54.4 at 5200 r.p.m.
Maximum torque: 63¾ft./lb. at 2600 r.p.m.
Rated h.p.: 10.9.
Firing order: 1, 3, 4, 2.
Contact-breaker gap: .010-.012in.
Spark-plug gap: .020-.022in.
Comp. pressure: 90lb./sq. in.
Ignition timing: TDC.

VALVES

Tappet clearance (all): .019in. hot.
Face angles: 30deg. all.
Valve timing:
    Inlet opens 11deg. BTDC.
    Exhaust closes 24deg. ATDC.
Valve overlap: 35deg.

CARBURATION

Twin SU'S, type H2.
Standard Needle: ES.
    Rich: EM.
    Weak: AP.
SU fuel pump, type L.

FRONT END

Caster: 8deg. (5½deg. on later models fitted with 2½deg. taper plates).
Camber: 3deg.
Toe-in: 3/16in.

TENS'ONS

Cylinder-head: 50ft./lb.
Main bearings: 63ft./lb.
Big-ends: 27ft./lb.

ures the centre bearing to the under block must be withdrawn completely (this screw is located between the distributor and the oil-sump aperture).

When the camshaft has been drawn sufficiently to bring the centre bearing free of its housing, the bearing must be removed from the camshaft, before withdrawal of the shaft can be completed.

When reassembling, make certain that the centre bearing is refitted with its matching holes in perfect alignment, so that the locating screw can be properly inserted (you could probe

with a blunt-end scriber to ensure that the screw will enter the bearing properly). After tightening, the screw should be wired to prevent it working loose.

Ignition Timing

Whenever the distributor has been removed, it is essential to retime the spark on refitting. To do this, first set the engine with pistons 1 and 4 on top dead centre. This is achieved when a hole in the outer flange of the crankshaft pulley lines up with a pointer on the block.

Now examine the valves to see whether the No. 1 or No. 4 piston is on its firing stroke. Turn the distributor shaft until the rotor is opposite the segment which has its spark plug cable leading to the "firing" cylinder, then insert the distributor. "Feel" it in until the nearest tooth engages, then turn the body about until the locking screw can enter, and lock it.

After checking that the points are gapped correctly, set the micrometer adjustment in the centre position, slack off the pinch-bolt and turn the distributor until the points are just breaking. This will give you a starting-point for finer tuning, which can only be carried out by testing the car on the road.

Remember, however, that fine tuning doesn't rely entirely on attention to the electrical system. The engine itself must be in good condition, and the compression readings on all cylinders within 5lb. of each other, before a fair degree of tune can be obtained.

Another — and possibly the most important — factor to consider (in view of the twin SU carburettors fitted to the TC) is carburation.

As well as tuning the carburettors, they must be synchronised to work together. The procedure is too long to be described here, but we ran a separate article on tuning twin SU's in the July 1960 issue of *Modern Motor*, to which you can refer if in doubt.

Clutch, Propeller Shaft

Access to the clutch for dismantling is obtained by removing the gearbox and clutch housing which is secured to the flywheel housing by a ring of bolts.

The clutch is removed from the flywheel as a complete unit by undoing the ring of bolts securing the clutch cover to the flywheel. To dismantle the clutch unit it is necessary only to remove the three nuts securing the clutch pressure plate by the fulcrum bolts to the clutch cover.

Usually the clutch finger adjustment is done on a special machine, but here's a tip on how to do the job easily. File three pieces of metal until they are exactly .285in. thick. Place them between the flywheel face and the pressure plate so that they are equally spaced (the clutch plate is, of course, removed while this is done). Bolt the clutch assembly to the flywheel and the fingers are ready for setting. With the flywheel flat on a bench, alter the screws until the height is exactly 1.665in. measured from the extreme tip of the finger to the face of the flywheel. This gives the exact setting.

The clutch pedal should have a minimum free travel of 1in. The stop limiting the travel of the pedal is then adjusted to give 3in. pedal movement after the 1in. free travel.

FAULT-FINDING CHART

● If engine will not start and starter will not crank engine, check for:
(a) Run-down battery
(b) Cable corroded or disconnected
(c) Faulty starter switch
(d) Dirty starter-drive assembly
(e) Broken drive spring
(f) Defective starter motor

● If the starter cranks the engine slowly but the engine will not start, check for:
(a) Loose terminals
(b) Dirty connections
(c) Battery charge low
(d) Faulty starter motor

● If the engine will not start and there is no spark at the plug gaps, check for oiled-up plugs or cracked porcelain.

● If there is no spark at the distributor plug leads, check for:
(a) Cracked rotor
(b) Loose low-tension wires
(c) Faulty cap
(d) Worn or dirty breaker points
(e) Faulty carbon-brush contact
(f) Defective condenser or connections

● If the ignition system is in order, check the fuel system; if there is no fuel in the carburettor, test for:
(a) Air leaks in the petrol line
(b) Blocked vent in petrol-tank cap
(c) Choked filters
(d) Blockage in the fuel pipe
(e) A faulty fuel pump

● If petrol is present but the trouble still seems to be due to a fuel fault, check for:
(a) Choked jets
(b) Defective starting control (choke)
(c) Air leak in induction manifold
(d) Water or dirt in the fuel

● If the engine misfires or runs imperfectly, it may be due to ignition defects as follows:
(a) High-tension lead shorting
(b) Distributor points not properly adjusted
(c) Defective or damp distributor cap

(d) Ignition timing incorrect
(e) Faulty condenser
(f) Cracked spark-plug porcelain, dirty or improperly gapped spark plugs
(g) Loose battery connection

● If ignition is not the cause of misfiring, check the fuel system for:
(a) Partly blocked fuel line or pump filter
(b) Float needle valve dirty or faulty
(c) Water in the carburettor
(d) Low pump pressure
(e) Carburettor flooding
(f) Weak mixture
(g) Blocked vent in petrol-tank cap

● Some mechanical factors which can cause misfiring or faulty running are:
(a) Excessive carbon deposit
(b) Sticking, burnt or broken valves
(c) Broken or weak valve springs
(d) Improper valve clearances

● If the engine starts and stops, check for:
(a) Loose connections in the low-tension circuit
(b) Faulty contact in the ignition switch
(c) Dirty contact points
(d) Defective condenser

● If this trouble is not due to faulty ignition, check for:
(a) Blocked fuel line
(b) Water or dirt in the fuel
(c) Lack of petrol
(d) Faulty fuel pump
(e) Air leaks in manifold system
(f) Sticking needle valve

● If the engine will not give full power, check for:
(a) Valves burnt or not seating properly
(b) Ignition retarded
(c) Automatic advance defective
(d) Defective high-tension leads or spark plugs
(e) Faulty distributor cap
(f) Insufficient fuel supply
(g) Air leaks in manifold system
(h) Jets partly blocked

These are the only adjustments possible to the clutch.

A Hardy Spicer needle-bearing type propeller shaft is fitted and each joint is filled with lubricant when assembled and a nipple is provided for subsequent lubrication. Should it be necessary to dismantle these joints, it can easily be accomplished by pinching together the ends of the retainer locking rings or circlips with a pair of pliers, and having removed them from their grooves, the bearings themselves can be tapped out from either side. When reassembling the joints, the bearings must be refilled with lubricant.

Before disconnecting the propeller shaft from the gearbox and rear axle flanges, it is extremely important to mark the adjacent flanges to ensure that the shaft retains its original relative positions on reassembly.

Should it be necessary to remove either the gearbox flange or rear axle flanges, it will also be necessary to mark these in relation to the primary shaft and pinion shaft, respectively, before removal. In addition, when removing these flanges, great care is necessary, as careless removal can so easily distort them, which completely destroys the concentricity of the propeller shaft. An ideal puller is one which will grip as large an area as close to the hubs as possible.

There is one additional point on

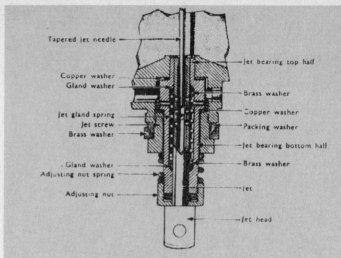

SECTION view of SU carburettor jet assembly.

In some cases, because of the lack of specialised equipment, it will not be possible for the owner to carry out some replacement and this should be done by a dealer equipped with necessary fixtures.

It is emphasised that there is no such thing as gear backlash figures, and quite apart from anything else, there is no way of checking this after assembly, as the housing has no inspection cover.

port from functioning and the brakes will probably bind. Lack of free movement can be caused by the pedal fouling the mats or floorboards, so this should also be checked.

To remove the master cylinder from the chassis, drain the supply tank by disconnecting the pipe at the main cylinder and depressing the pedal slowly by hand, allowing the fluid to drain into a clean container.

Repeat this until the tank is drained, then detach the pushrod from the foot pedal. Remove the nut which holds the cylinder to the chassis and withdraw the cylinder.

To draw the piston from the cylinder, take out the spring circlip inside the end of the cylinder. This circlip acts as the piston stop or limiting point and after the piston is removed, the rubber cup, spring and valve are readily removable.

When cleaning brake parts, never use petrol, kerosene or oil, as they are likely to contaminate the rubber parts either during overhaul or later on after assembly. Only brake fluid should be used for this purpose.

To adjust the brakes, jack up one wheel and working on the backing plate you will find two hexagon headed screws situated a few inches down and on each side of the plate below the point where the flexible brake hose screws into the plate. Adjustment is made by rotating the adjustment cam A (see illustration) against stop pin B on the shoe. Rotate the adjustment nut C with a wrench until the brake comes into contact with the drum, then back off slightly until the wheel rotates freely. One complete turn of nut C is sufficient to take up all lining wear, so when adjusting, the nut will only require a partial turn before the shoes are brought in contact with the drum. The same procedure is carried out on the other wheels.

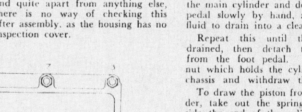

TIGHTENING sequence for cylinder-head nuts.

the propeller shaft which requires lubrication and this is the splined shaft at the forward end, and a grease nipple is provided for this purpose.

Rear Axle

No adjustment is provided for the crown wheel and pinion or bearings except by distance pieces which are all accurately marked with their thickness. All components are marked with a plus or minus figure, indicating in thousandths of an inch the variation from the nominal dimension. Special tools are needed for some replacements. Provided the replacements have the same markings as the originals, it is possible to replace the crown wheel and pinion or the nearside axle casing or differential bearing.

Servicing Brakes

Brakes are of the Lockheed hydraulic type and to obtain greater braking power on the front wheels, the diameter of the front wheel cylinders is greater than those at the rear.

The master cylinder is of the combination barrel compensating type which provides automatic compensation for expansion or contraction of the fluid due to temperature changes. For correct brake pedal adjustment, it is important that the master cylinder pushrod has a slight clearance where it fits into the cup of the piston when it is in the off position. If the rod is tight against the piston, the by-pass port may be covered by the master cup washer. This will prevent the compensating

MODERN MOTOR — January 1961

AS SHE IS: *winning Class F sprint at Strathpine last year, with present owner Bob Burnett at the wheel.*

200,000 MILES, FOUR OWNERS

modern MOTOR SPECIAL TEST

— yet this 1946 TC still runs like a watch and wins contests, says ex-owner David McKay

WHEN you've owned a good car, you always retain a sentimental affection for it — so it was a great pleasure to renew the acquaintance of a green TC which I had owned and raced some years ago.

Pleasure turned to delight when I heard that the 12-year-old car, with 200,000 miles on the clock, had won the last two Concours d'Elegance conducted by the Queensland MG Car Club, and was still fast enough to score an occasional race or sprint victory.

Quite a feat for any MG of that vintage — but a truly amazing effort for a car which had always been driven hard, never underwent a major renovation, and most of the time combined the life of an everyday "bread-and-butter" buggy with competition at weekends.

News of its latest successes came from present owner Bob Burnett, who visited Sydney recently and called in to give me a look at the old car — and to ask if I'd like to give it a test, just for the hell of it.

FIRST BLOWER was fitted in 1946, when car was only a few weeks old. With 4.8:1 rear end and 19-inch wheels, it gave TC a genuine 100 m.p.h.

Test it I did — and found the old-timer as sprightly as ever, as you'll see from the performance figures. But first, let's review the TC's chequered career.

First Post-war Lot

The story begins in 1946, when Cowra (N.S.W.) grazier Tony Fagan bought one of the first shipment of six post-war MG's to arrive in Sydney. Price was around £620 and all the cars were black; this one had red trim and the registered number TK233.

Tony's elder brother was driving a 4.3 Alvis at the time and regularly winning the Cowra-Sydney G.P. when the graziers came to town. Tony tired of running second and had Rex Marshall, of the now defunct Monza Motors, fit a "blower" to the TC; but apart from a small boost gauge there was no outward sign of the considerably increased horsepower this put beneath the classic bonnet

AS SHE WAS when McKay had her: above, stripped down for her first race (Bathurst, October, 1950); below, semi-stripped for hill-climbing. McKay won 1951 N.S.W. sports hillclimb title in this TC.

From that day the big Alvis had to tail the TC, which could turn up a genuine 100 m.p.h. with a 4.8 final drive and 500 by 19in. tyres.

Fagan also had the car reduced by Sydney craftsman Henry Stahl in two beautiful shades of green, which are as good today as they were 12 years ago. But then he fell in love with a 3½-litre SS100 Jag, and the MG passed to me for £600 plus a well-used pre-war Anglia.

In 18 months Tony had run up about 25,000 hard and fast miles, but the car had always been scrupulously maintained and immaculately kept. He later told me the SS100 was no substitute for the blown TC.

Racing Career Starts

Between 1948 and 1950 I used the car as fast transport between Exeter and Warrawee — just on 100 miles from door to door, covered on one

MAIN SPECIFICATIONS

ENGINE: 4-cylinder, o.h.v.; bore 70 mm., stroke 90 mm., capacity 1398 c.c.; compression ratio 8.3 to 1; maximum b.h.p. 58 at 5800 r.p.m.; twin 1½in. SU carburettors.

TRANSMISSION: Single dry-plate clutch; 4-speed, fully-synchromeshed gearbox; final drive ratio 5.1 to 1; 15.8 m.p.h. per 1000 r.p.m. in top gear.

SUSPENSION: Solid beam axle in front, with transverse leaf spring; semi-elliptics at rear; hydraulic shock-absorbers all round.

STEERING: High-geared cam type; 1½ turns lock-to-lock; 40ft. turning circle.

WHEELS: Wire, with knock-on hubs; tyres, front 500 by 16in., rear 600 by 16in.

WEIGHT (as tested): 17½ cwt.

FUEL TANK: 13½ gallons.

PERFORMANCE ON TEST

BEST SPEED: 94 m.p.h.

FLYING quarter-mile: 90 m.p.h.

STANDING quarter-mile: 21.8s.

ACCELERATION through gears: 0-30,

5s.; 0-40, 8s.; 0-50, 11.8s.; 0-60, 18s.; 0-70, 23s.

BRAKING: 95 percent efficient—no fade.

CONSUMPTION: 28 m.p.g. overall.

200,000 MILES, FOUR OWNERS

...lorious dawn run in 1hr. 45min. ...ack in town' I found the blower ...ather fussy and sold it.

The car was serviced all this time ...y Rex Marshall, who prepared Jack ...aywell's racers, and so it was natural ...he bug would bite me. I got Rex ...o prepare the MG for the October, ...950, Bathurst meeting.

She was stripped; lights, seats and ...o on were all carefully preserved ...ith wax and sheeting. The tune was ...uild at 9.3 to 1 on 100-octane, which ...ame by courtesy of Kingsford Smith ...erodrome.

I thoroughly enjoyed myself at the ...eeting. She ran like a clock and ...nished eighth in the under-1500 c.c. ...0-mile scratch race—enough to whet ...y appetite.

From then on the car was raced, ...printed and hill-climbed at most ...ajor N.S.W. meetings. During a ...leasant 10 days in Victoria we made ...astest "unblown" 1500 c.c. sports-car ...me at Rob Roy, then ran second ...o Harry Firth's MG Special at Balla-...at, disposing of a brace of XK's on ...he way.

By this time Ron Ward was in ...harge of preparation. In 1951 we ...on the N.S.W. 1500c.c. sports hill-...limb title at Hawkesbury and would ...ave scored again the following year ...t Newcastle if the organisers hadn't ...aken exception to the TC's cycle ...uards and classified it as "racing," ...ot "sports."

Throughout these years the car ...erved as my personal transport ...round town, topping 45,000 miles on ...he clock. In addition, its competition ...fe could be assessed at 5000 miles—...he equivalent of 25,000 road miles.

Then I started racing another MG, ...nown as the "Red Cigar." The green ...ar became her tender and mobile ...pares storeroom, having such things ...s axles, brake drums, wheels, tyres ...nd final-drive units torn from her ...t a moment's notice by Gordon ...tewart, who maintained the red ...acer throughout its very successful ...952-53 season.

Toppled Record

But the green TC wasn't through ...ith racing yet.

In fact, the highlight of her career ...as the production-car race at Bath-...rst, following the 1952 Australian ...P.

The race was in two sections, sports ...nd saloons, and entries had to be ...rictly standard except for compres-...on ratio. This, however, was limited ...y the compulsory use of standard ...etrol—about 72 octane in those days. Before the TC was accepted, I had ...remove the finned brake drums, en-

...larged sump, and the rods which pre-vent the front axle twisting under severe braking; they also told me to cut all binding from the cam springs fore and aft, disconnect the oil-tem-perature gauge, and even replace the K3-type radiator filler cap!

The car had to use 19in. wheels and have normal 5.12 axle ratio—in short, it had to be exactly as sold back in 1946, with the exception of a carefully matched 8.3 to 1 head, the work of Charlie Buck.

Finally everything was in order and I had finished the GP in the "Cigar" when the production race was on, and had my eye fairly well in after 38 laps of the Mt. Panorama circuit.

The green car seemed rejuvenated at the prospect of racing again. It covered the six laps in fine style, al-though the water was at 100deg. C. after the first ascent of the mountain. Best lap for a standard TC had been around four minutes, but our timers clocked the car at under 3.50 every lap, with a best time of 3.45. As far as I know, this has never been equalled by a similar car.

The TC won the sports section from Jack Robinson's fast-approaching XK120, and just failed to catch the winning saloon, an incredible Citroen 15 driven by Bill Buckle.

Midway through 1953 I regretfully sold "old faithful" to Sydney archi-tect Bruce Shaw for about £700. Its condition and reputation were such that it commanded this price when 1946 TC's were selling for as low as £450.

Cheap Motoring

Apart from racing expenses, which ran into four figures, the car had cost remarkably little to keep. It had covered a total of 120,000 miles in its seven-year grind; now, as a reward, it was retired from active competition.

Shaw used it as a daily hack; he used to take his holidays on Queens-land's "Gold Coast," and the green car carried him there and back swiftly and economically.

Towards the end of his "tenancy" Shaw hankered for more speed, so he had a big blower fitted to the engine by Bob Pritchett.

Like Fagan and myself before him, Shaw met his wife and courted her with the aid of the TC, and when he finally sold the car it was to pur-chase a Peugeot, as I had done.

In four years, the car had cost Shaw £700, which included the cost of the blower and a gearbox overhaul, in-surance, tyres, repairs and running ex-penses. At £175 a year for another 70,000 miles, that was cheap motor-ing!

Sold to Queensland

Bob Burnett, a foundation member of the Q.R.D.C., now comes into the picture. Seeing the TC in Queen-land on one of Shaw's periodical visits, he earmarked it for himself—and when Shaw was ready to sell, Burnett snapped it up.

Now he has these two Concours d'Elegance to his credit, a further 10,-000 miles on the log, and a victory at a Strathpine sprint meeting with a standing-quarter time of 18.2 sec. in full road trim.

Bob overhauled the motor 5000 miles back, but this still has all the original major components such as crankshaft, rods, pistons and head; and the transmission is so obviously sound that Bob doubts whether he'll bother looking at it.

Test at 200,000

When Bob offered me the car for testing, I considered its age and mileage and doubted if I should give the full treatment. But Bob insisted that she'd be able to take it—and he was right.

The blower was temporarily off, and the engine was fitted with two 1½in. carbies; otherwise everything looked just as before. Duco, leather uphols-tery and wooden dash were in excel-lent condition and the engine healthy and willing—certainly no noisier than I remembered it, despite fairly wide tappet settings.

Acceleration times may not be startling by modern standards, but they're excellent when you consider the car's long, eventful history. The Kurrajong climb time was particu-larly good, equalling that of the Aus-tin A95, which is no mean climber with a 50 m.p.h. second gear. She was certainly puffing a bit at the sum-mit, but didn't boil as some modern cars have done when climbed hard.

With 16in. tyres and low pressures, the TC rode remarkably well and the steering was accurate and light at speed—rather better than I imagined, and due, I think, to a recent thor-ough overhaul by Burnett. We covered nearly 200 fast miles and the car stood up to it better than I—this driver was frankly weary, being spoiled for this type of motoring by modern suspension.

But then, this sort of car offers an experience no enthusiast should miss. Not to have driven a good TC is like visiting London and not seeing Big Ben—something lacking in one's edu-cation.

Whatever lies ahead for the green car, it's nice to know she's in good hands. Queenslanders have recently offered £750 for her unsuccessfully—it's unlikely she'll be available before she's snared her fourth bride! ● ●

KNOW YOUR MG TD

THE TD series M.G., first produced in January 1950, replaced the earlier TC. The later model closely followed the series Y 1¼ litre saloon, using the same type of independent external coil front suspension with piston type shock absorbers and rack and pinion steering.

The box section chassis frame was slightly different from the saloon, being upswept over the rear axle to provide greater clearance between the underframe and ground. Although the body design is not much different, one distinguishable feature is perforated disc wheels, whereas the TC was fitted with wire wheels.

The chassis serial number, which will be found on the front extension of the chassis frame on the nearside, just behind the front bumperbar holding stud and on a plate on the near side of the scuttle under the bonnet, commenced at TD0251.

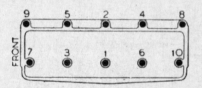

HEAD tightening sequence for TD.

Engine numbers started at 501 and have the prefix XPAG/TD. A 2 follows the prefix at engine No. 9408 to indicate some major changes, which include a larger clutch, 8in. instead of 7½in., a new flywheel, bell housing and clutch cross shaft.

A further change occurring at engine No. 2/14224 was a new oil pump assembly which had the pump and filter combined. This assembly is interchangeable with earlier models. A little later at engine No. 2/14948, the sump was altered, the front step

being done away with and the oil capacity increased.

The threads and hexagons used throughout are a mixture. On some models, metric and B.S.F. threads are employed, using Whitworth hexagons. Some later models use SAE threads and hexagons on the front and rear axles.

Engine Mountings

The engine is mounted at the front by a bonded rubber block, which is bolted to the front cross member and to a "U" bracket on the front engine plate. At the rear, the extension from the gearbox rests on two loose blocks in the frame cradle. A forked bolt, pinned to a lug on the gearbox, projects downward through the cradle and rebound rubber bush, and a cup washer with the edge facing downwards fits between the nut and the rubber. The nut should only be tightened enough to insert the split pin.

A fore and aft transverse link fitted between the front of the engine and the bracket on the chassis takes torque reaction. The link is anchored in rubber at both ends, and is fitted with a turnbuckle for adjustment.

When the engine has been taken out and refitted, refit the link before the exhaust system is connected. Make sure the engine is quite free by rocking it slightly so that it will assume a natural and neutral position on the mountings.

The link should now be lengthened until the inner rubbers at each end bear lightly but firmly on brackets without altering the position of the engine. The outer rubbers should now be fitted and the nuts tightened just sufficient to "nip" the rubbers.

Removing the Engine

There are two methods of removing the engine—either complete with

gearbox or the engine alone, with gearbox remaining in position. The gearbox can also be taken out as a unit, leaving the engine in place, as explained farther on.

To take out the engine only, take off all usual components such as

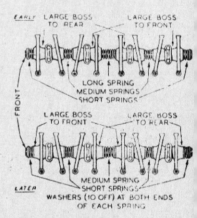

TWO types of valve rocker gear have been used on the TD series.

bonnet, hoses and headlamp brackets from shell. Remove radiator core and shell together, disconnect all pipes, wires, controls and torque "fore and aft" link. Take off oil filter, starter motor, and gearbox cowl. Now take the engine weight with slings, detach the front mounting from the engine bracket and place a jack under the gearbox to take weight. Remove all set-screws around the bell housing and draw engine forwards and upwards.

When reassembling take note of the rubber buffers on the studs below the radiator core. These studs are shouldered and the nuts should be fully tightened.

MODERN MOTOR—December 1956

Bearings, Oil Seals

The engine must be completely removed and stripped if the main bearings need replacing, because the main bearing shells, which are of thick steel lined with white metal, are dowelled into both the caps and block. Crankshaft end float is controlled by the centre main bearing flanged on both sides.

No hand fitting of the bearings is permitted and for this reason the shaft should be ground to the standard undersizes of $\frac{1}{2}$ or 1 mm.

The flywheel spigot bearing is a bushed type pressed into the end of the crankshaft. The timing sprocket and fan pulley are keyed separately to the front end of the shaft and have an oil thrower fitted between. The assembly is kept on by the crank handle dog set screw. Oil sealing at the front end is accomplished by using a split composition seal located in the nose of the sump and in a groove in the timing cover. When fitting new seals, both halves should stand slightly proud. At the rear, the wall of the sump fits around the rear main bearing cap with cork strips in the cap groove.

The ends of the cork sump gasket must fit over the ends of both front and rear seals. Also at the rear a

crankshaft oil return thread spins in a split collector housing with the lower half cast in the sump and the upper half dowelled and bolted to the crankshaft. The ends of these housings must ˙butt together, and jointing compound should be applied to the faces before joining them. It is possible to fit new rings without removing the head, as the

VALVE timing and dwell are clearly seen in this diagram.

piston and con-rod assembly are withdrawn downwards past the crankshaft webs.

When reassembling, make sure that the piston pin clamp bolts are on the opposite side to the camshaft.

The duplex timing chain is of the endless type, and if removal is desired the sprockets must be removed.

Camshaft Removal

The three camshaft bearings are replaceable, the centre (split type) and rear bush are located by set-screws and the front bush is a tight press fit. To control camshaft end float, a thrust plate is placed between the timing sprocket and a shoulder on the camshaft and bolted to the crankcase.

Removal of the camshaft can be carried out without taking the engine from the frame by using the following procedure: Detach the front mounting and raise the engine slightly to enable the oil pump to be removed. Take off the radiator, sump, timing cover, chain and sprockets, oil pump, distributor, rocker gear, push-rods and tappets. Now detach the thrust plate and the bearing locating set-screws. The shaft can now be drawn out a little, bringing the split centre bearing with it. Take out this bearing when the shaft is about halfway out.

MG TD   FAULT-FINDING CHART

● If engine will not start and starter will not crank engine, check for:
(a) Run-down battery
(b) Cable corroded or disconnected
(c) Faulty starter switch
(d) Dirty starter-drive assembly
(e) Broken drive spring
(f) Defective starter motor

● If the starter cranks the engine slowly but the engine will not start, check for:
(a) Loose terminals
(b) Dirty connections
(c) Battery charge low
(d) Faulty starter motor

● If the engine will not start and there is no spark at the plug gaps, check for oiled-up plugs or cracked porcelain.

● If there is no spark at the distributor plug leads, check for:
(a) Cracked rotor
(b) Loose low-tension wires
(c) Faulty cap
(d) Worn or dirty breaker points
(e) Faulty carbon-brush contact
(f) Defective condenser or connections

● If the ignition system is in order, check the fuel system; if there is no fuel in the carburettor, test for:
(a) Air leaks in the petrol line
(b) Blocked vent in petrol-tank cap
(c) Choked filters

(d) Blockage in the fuel pipe
(e) A faulty fuel pump

● If petrol is present but the trouble still seems to be due to a fuel fault, check for:
(a) Choked jets
(b) Defective starting control (choke)
(c) Air leak in induction manifold
(d) Water or dirt in the fuel

● If the engine misfires or runs imperfectly, it may be due to ignition defects as follow:
(a) High-tension lead shorting
(b) Distributor points not properly adjusted
(c) Defective or damp distributor cap
(d) Ignition timing incorrect
(e) Faulty condenser
(f) Cracked spark-plug porcelain, dirty or improperly gapped spark plugs
(g) Loose battery connection

● If ignition is not the cause of misfiring, check the fuel system for:
(a) Partly blocked fuel line or pump filter
(b) Float needle valve dirty or faulty
(c) Water in the carburettor
(d) Low pump pressure
(e) Carburettor flooding
(f) Weak mixture
(g) Blocked vent in petrol-tank cap

● Some mechanical factors which can cause misfiring or faulty running are:
(a) Excessive carbon deposit
(b) Sticking, burnt or broken valves
(c) Broken or weak valve springs
(d) Improper valve clearances

● If the engine starts and stops, check for:
(a) Loose connections in the low-tension circuit
(b) Faulty contact in the ignition switch
(c) Dirty contact points
(d) Defective condenser

● If this trouble is not due to faulty ignition, check for:
(a) Blocked fuel line
(b) Water or dirt in the fuel
(c) Lack of petrol
(d) Faulty fuel pump
(e) Air leaks in manifold system
(f) Sticking needle valve

● If the engine will not give full power, check for:
(a) Valves burnt or not seating properly
(b) Ignition retarded
(c) Automatic advance defective
(d) Defective high-tension leads or spark plugs
(e) Faulty distributor cap
(f) Insufficient fuel supply
(g) Air leaks in manifold system
(h) Jets partly blocked

To obtain the correct valve timing, the sprockets and chain should be positioned so as to make the bright links of the chain correspond with "T" marks stamped on the sprockets, with the shorter run of the chain (between the bright links) towards the top of the engine. The camshaft and crankshaft keyways should be turned so that they correspond with the keyways in the gears.

Inlet and exhaust guides are of different lengths, the inlet being the longer. They are pressed into the head until the outsides of the guides are projecting exactly 24 mm. above the face of the head.

To avoid confusion when reassembling the rocker arms, they should be identified before removal.

There are two variations in rocker-arm assemblies, as shown in the accompanying sketch. The early type were used up to engine No. XPAG/TD9007. Later, the modified boss type were used for the exhaust rockers.

Distributor, Carburettor

The ignition system uses a distributor which revolves anti-clockwise with the centrifugal advance mechanism spigoted in the crankcase on the near side and retained by a clamp-plate and dowel-ended set-screws. A skew driven gear is pinned to the distributor shaft and is driven by the camshaft. The contact breaker points should be set to open when the engine is at t.d.c. A hole drilled in the

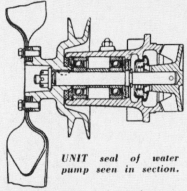

UNIT seal of water pump seen in section.

crankshaft pulley and a pointer on the timing cover give this position. Final adjustment is made by road test. Distributor advance commences at 460 to 800 r.p.m., reaching a maximum of 28 to 32 crankshaft degrees at 4400 r.p.m. The cam angle is 49 deg., plus or minus 4 deg. Carburettors are twin SU horizontal (H2) using standard needles type ES. If richer or leaner needles are required, use EM for rich and AP for lean. Average fuel pump pressure is ¾lb. to 1lb. p.s.i.

Water Pump Overhaul

The cooling system is pump pressure type with a bellows thermostat in a housing bolted to the elbow on

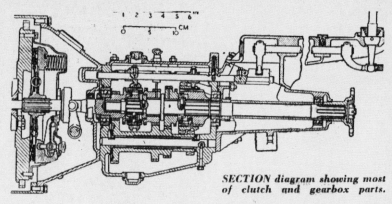

SECTION diagram showing most of clutch and gearbox parts.

front of the cylinder head. Early model pumps used spring loaded rubber and carbon seals, while later pumps used unit type seals (see diagram).

To remove the pump, the radiator must first be taken off. To dismantle the pump, tap out the tapered pin and draw off the impellor with spring, rubber seal and carbon disc. Be careful not to lose the disc driving peg, which is loose in the shaft. On later model pumps, the seal assembly is pressed into the body and a washer is interposed between the carbon face and the impellor. Extract the split pin (a pair of long pliers will be found right for this) and undo the pulley nut, then draw off the pulley with felt seal and retainer. Prise out the spring ring which holds the outer section of the front ball-bearing, then tap the end of the shaft on a wooden block until the bearing comes out. Next, extract the spring ring which fits in a groove of the housing behind the front race and draw out the shaft complete with the rear race and felt oil retainer.

When reassembling, note that the flat, rearmost retainer has a tongue which engages a keyway in the shaft. The outer edge of the dished retainer fits against the felt seal.

Fan-belt adjustment is by swinging the generator bracket until there is ½in. free play on the long run of the belt.

Clutch Adjustment

The Borg and Beck single-plate clutch uses a graphite type release bearing. No external adjustment is possible, except from pedal travel and free movement, which should be ¾in. and ⅛in. respectively. To work on the clutch, the gearbox and bell housing will first have to be removed (described later).

Usually the clutch finger adjustment is done on a special machine, but here's a tip on how to do the job easily. File three pieces of metal until they are exactly .285in. thick. Place them between the flywheel face and the pressure plate so that they are equally spaced (the clutch plate is, of course, removed while this is done). Bolt the clutch assembly to

the flywheel and the fingers are now ready for setting. With the flywheel flat on a bench, alter the screws until the height is exactly 1.665in. measured from the extreme tip of the finger to the face of the flywheel. This gives the exact setting.

To remove the gearbox, take out the carpets, cowling and floorboards, undo the spedeo cable and the clutch rod, take out the two set-screws which hold the exhaust pipe bracket to the gearbox, take off the nut and cup washer, followed by the rubber bush below the rear mounting. Lift the gearbox a little, and take out the clevis pin from the forked bolt. Jack up the rear of the engine to take the weight, then remove the ten screws around the bell-housing flange and detach the clutch inspection cover. (When refitting the cover, note that the air vent goes towards the driving side.) The gearbox can now be drawn back carefully and lifted off. Replacement is the reverse.

Dismantling the Gearbox

To dismantle the gearbox, take off the bell housing, top cover and the gearbox extension cover with the remote control. Then pick out the selector springs. Undo the large nut at the rear and draw off the flange which drives the propeller shaft. Remove the spedeo drive housing and take out the square head set-screws from the selector rods used to locate three striking jaws at the rear, the three selector forks, the stop for the first and second gears (at front end on offside) and the reverse rod steady.

On later models the centre rod has a spring ring at the front end and this acts as a stop.

Undo the rear extension housing nuts and draw the housing back until the striking jaws can be taken off. The housing can then be removed and the selector rods drawn out. Take out the middle rod last with the interlock plunger (which is pegged in place). There are five balls to be caught or retrieved. These are identical in size—three are the selector balls and two interlock balls. A set-screw below the rear of the box is used to lock the layshaft spindle in

TUNING DATA

Firing order: 1, 3, 2, 4.
Comp. pressure: 90lb.
Oil pressure: 60lb.
Bore and stroke: 66½ x 90mm.
Comp. ratio: 7.25:1.
Rated h.p.: 10.9.
B.h.p.: 54.4 at 5200 r.p.m.
Contact points: .012.
Spark plugs: .020-022.

VALVES

Tappets (hot): .019 both.
Face and seat angles: 30 deg.
Spring test, inner: 1.438in. at 43lb. **Outer:** 1.532in. at 80lb.

CARBURETTOR

Float level: 3/8in. bar under fork.
Needle, standard: ES.
Richer, EM, leaner, AP.
Fuel pump pressure: ¾-1lb.

VOLTAGE REGULATOR

Air gap: .012-020.
Point gap: .006-.017.
Cut out closes at 12.7-13.3 v.

FRONT END

Caster (fixed): 2 deg., plus or minus ¼ deg.
Camber (fixed): 1 deg.
Toe-in (adjustable): Nil.

TENSIONS

Cylinder head: 50 ft./lb.
Main bearings: 63.
Big ends: 27.

the casing. This must be removed before attempting to punch or drift the spindle rearwards.

After the latter is done, the cluster will drop into the bottom of the housing. Now drive the main shaft forward to push out the primary (or clutch) shaft, together with its ball bearing. By punching or drifting from the inside the rear ball race can be removed. This will allow the mainshaft to be tilted and lifted out through the top opening. To dismantle the mainshaft assembly, slide off the 3rd and 4th speed synchromesh assembly as a unit. On later model boxes one hole is drilled right through the hub and an extra ball inserted under the spring, dropping into a notch in the mainshaft. Catch the spring and two balls as they are released.

Depress the plunger, locating the splined thrust washer in the 3rd gear cone, then turn the washer a little and slide it off. This will free the 3rd gear and needle rollers. Now extract the spring ring and slide off the 2nd gear synchro unit. Depress the 2nd gear backing plunger with a wire passed through the hole in the collar, and remove the splined collar and split thrust washer followed by the 2nd gear and needle rollers which are drawn off. On later cars, the synchro sleeves can be slid off their

hubs without the balls springing out, as they are peened into their holes.

When reassembling, a dummy layshaft should be made up, otherwise it will be almost impossible to keep the needle rollers and thrust washers in place. The dummy shaft is made from 9/16in. diameter rod and should be exactly 6 11/32in. long. This is inserted in the cluster first, and after feeding in the 28 rollers (14 each end) place the thrust washers and tabbed collars (boss towards the rollers and passing through the washers) at each end. The complete assembly can then be dropped into the gearbox and the tabs on the collars arranged to register with slots in the casting. Thirty-two rollers are used on third gear and the mainshaft, 28 on the 2nd gear and 18 for the main drive pocket. . These are kept in place by fibrous grease during assembly (106 rollers in all).

Rear Axle, Hubs

On early models, the rear hubs were serviced as an assembly with brake drums, and these should not be separated. On later models, the hub and drum are cast as a unit and fitted on splines on the axle half shafts. Split collars are pulled up against the hubs with a large axle nut. A ball race is spigoted into the housing, fitting in about half way, and the bearing housing (which carries an oil seal with the lip towards the race) bolts up to the flanged end of the axle housing with the brake backing plate, to effectively seal and retain the shaft and race in position.

To remove an axle shaft, draw off the hub, remove the brake backing plate assembly, then slip off the split conical collar. An impulse puller is generally used to withdraw the axle; however, if not available, screw on the hub nut with a large washer and tap this evenly around and the shaft should come out together with the bearing housing, oil seal, and ball bearing.

If a new bearing is to be pressed on to the shaft, do not omit the spacing ring used to cover the fillet or radius on the shaft and provide a flat area for the race to press against. When refitting each component, tap all round with a hide-faced hammer to ensure correct seating before locking up the assembly.

No adjustment is provided for the crown wheel and pinion or bearings except by distance pieces which are all accurately marked with their thickness. All components are marked with a plus or minus figure, indicating in thousandths of an inch the variation from the nominal dimension. Special tools are needed for some replacements. Provided the replacements have the same markings as the originals, it is possible to replace the crown wheel and pinion or the nearside axle casing or differential bearing.

In some cases, because of the lack of specialised equipment, it will not be possible for the owner to carry out some replacement and this should be done by a dealer equipped with necessary fixtures.

It is emphasised that there is no such thing as gear backlash figures, and quite apart from anything else, there is no way of checking this after assembly, as the housing has no inspection cover.

Brake Adjustment

The Lockheed hydraulic brake system uses two leading shoes on the front wheels with a separate wheel cylinder for each shoe. The rear brakes have one wheel cylinder only. This is a floating type which carries a ball crank lever for operating the handbrake through separate cables. To take up lining wear, a "Micram" adjuster is fitted to each wheel cylinder. The slotted head of the adjuster is reached through a hole in the drum, after the wheel is removed.

These adjusters (two for the front wheels and one in each rear wheel) should be turned in a clockwise direction until the shoe just touches the drum, then backed off one notch. Don't interfere with the adjusting nuts on the cable ends at the base of the handbrake lever unless new cables are to be fitted. The cables should be just without tension when the brakes are off.

Front Suspension

It is important to note that the near-side king pin and stub axle have left-hand threads. To dismantle the suspension, jack up the chassis until the front wheels are clear, then jack up separately under each spring pad until the upper wishbone is clear of the rebound rubber. Disconnect the tie rods by releasing the lock nuts and unscrewing the rods from the outer ball sockets. Disconnect the brake flexible hoses from the chassis unions and take out the suspension outer pivot bolts, the stub axle, king pin, and pivot lug assembly. Lower the jacks under the coil springs, then press down the lower links and take out the springs. The rubber bush assemblies are similar to those of the rear spring shackles.

The upper links are removed with the shock absorbers. There are two set-screws and two bolts inserted from below, through the spring abutment. Note the flat portions on the bolt heads which are used to register with the edge of the spring locating plate through which the bolts pass.

To lock the king pins, the steering arms are used as a locating medium. Piston lugs which screw on to the king pins are free to turn without fouling the latter by waisting, i.e., a grooved area is machined at the top and bottom of the king pins.

When reassembling, see that the stub axles swivel fully before hooking up the tie-rods. ● ● ●

MG TF

TECHNICAL DATA

ENGINE: 4-cylinder o.h.v.; bore 66.5mm.; stroke 90mm.; capacity 1250 c.c.; compression ratio 8 to 1; rated b.h.p. 10.97; maximum b.h.p. 57½ at 5500 r.p.m.; road speed at 2500ft. per min. piston speed 65 m.p.h.; road speed at 1000 r.p.m. in top gear 15.3 m.p.h.; twin 1½in; S.U. carburettors fitted; S.U. electric fuel pump; ignition 12-volt; full-flow oil filter.

TRANSMISSION: 8in. single dry-plate clutch; four-speed gearbox with synchromesh on top three ratios; gear ratios 17.06, 10.09, 6.725, and 4.875 to 1, reverse 17.06 to 1; central floor control gear-change lever; rear axle with hypoid final drive; open propeller shaft.

SUSPENSION: Independent front-wheel suspension with coil springs and wishbones; semi-elliptic springs at rear; hydraulic piston-type dampers front and rear.

CHASSIS: Full chassis with boxed side frames and tubular cross-members.

BRAKES: Lockheed hydraulic, with 2 leading shoes in front; 115 sq. in. of lining area per ton. Handbrake operates mechanically on rear wheels from lever between seats.

TANKS: Petrol 12 gal., including 2½ gal. reserve; sump 10½ pints; radiator 10¾ pints.

STEERING: Rack-and-pinion; 2 2/3 turns lock-to-lock; turning circle 31ft.

WHEELS: Rudge Whitworth wire wheels with knock-off centre caps; 5.50in. x 15in. tyres.

DIMENSIONS: Wheelbase 7ft. 10in.; track front 4ft. 3/16in.; track rear 4ft. 2 13/16in.; overall length 12ft. 3in.; overall width 4ft. 11¾in.; height with hood up 4ft. 4½in.; ground clearance 6in.

WEIGHT: 17¼ cwt.; as tested 20¾ cwt.

PERFORMANCE FIGURES

BEST SPEED: 88.2 m.p.h. or 10 1/5 seconds over the measured quarter-mile.

MEAN of three opposite runs over the quarter-mile: 86.5 m.p.h., or 10 2/3 seconds.

STANDING quarter mile: 19 4/5 seconds.

ACCELERATION from rest through gears: 0 to 30 m.p.h., 4 s.; 0 to 40, 8 s.; 0 to 50, 12 s.; 0 to 60, 15 2/5 s.; 0 to 70, 30 s.

ACCELERATION in top gear: 10 to 30 m.p.h., 8 s.; 20 to 40, 10 s.; 30 to 50, 11 3/5 s.; 40 to 60, 11 s.

MAXIMUM SPEEDS in gears: First 26 m.p.h.; second 46; third 66.

DISTANCE of test course: 158 miles.

CONDITIONS for test: Fine; approx 10 m.p.h. cross-wind.

FUEL used: Standard pump petrol.

PETROL CONSUMPTION, including all test runs: 26.2 m.p.g.

TRIP and full mileage recorder was found accurate.

PRICE

£982 including tax.

A DAY at the wheel of the latest MG TF can be summed up in two words—magnificent motoring. Where sports cars are concerned MG is a household word; it is the small car with the big performance. I say without reserve that this new TF, with its lively power unit and excellent road manners, is the best yet from the MG factory.

Streamlining and certain alterations to body shape have not changed the traditional MG character—one that finds a warm place in the hearts of sports-car enthusiasts. Wire wheels and knock-off hub caps have been restored with this model; their return will be especially popular in Australia.

During the test, which took place on varied road surfaces, I found that the car handled beautifully; the controls were well placed and the driving position excellent. Lowering the frontal area has greatly improved the driver's immediate vision. Increase of maximum b.h.p. from 54 to 57½, better-breathing, the use of a higher compression ratio of 8 to 1, and the fitting of larger-bore carburettors have all contributed to improved performance in general, as the test figures show.

Road Behavior

Silent in operation over even the worst road surfaces, the independent front suspension gives a firm ride—and more comfort than some saloon cars tested. The seats are large and comfortable. I was able to drive the car over a rather twisting and undulating 11 miles of highway in under 10 minutes, during which it

Performer

handled to perfection. The time taken could even have been less. Rear suspension is by semi-elliptic springs; the Armstrong double-action piston-type shock-absorbers provide excellent stability.

Round fast corners with the speedometer needle hovering around 88 m.p.h., there is a slight tendency to drift. Under power this can be corrected effortlessly. Adhesion is excellent, and tyre squeal and body roll are almost non-existent. Downhill S-bends were taken rapidly, on the correct line. Breakaway from the rear wheels is considerably less than with the previous model, and very little correction is required. The car responds accurately at all times.

Even over corrugated, unsealed sections adhesion is good, and very little correction is needed when the rear end does break away on these surfaces.

Steering and Brakes

As on the TD, rack-and-pinion steering gear is employed, which is extremely accurate and allows high-speed touring. I could not detect any sign of under- or over-steer. The steering wheel is adjustable on the column and is comparatively "naked." It needs 2 2/3rd turns to take you from lock to lock. The turning circle is 31ft. Some road shock is transmitted to the steering wheel, but damping has reduced this as compared with the earlier model.

MODERN MOTOR — July 1954

T. F. ROAD TEST

Plus

—that's how Barrie Louden sums up the new TF model MG. Here is his report.

INSTRUMENTS are grouped in centre of dash with glovebox on either side. **FRONT SUSPENSION,** of independent coil-spring wishbone type, offers comfortable but firm ride. **CHASSIS FRAME** sweeps over hypoid rear axle to give low centre of gravity.

MODERN MOTOR — July 1954

MG TF ROAD TEST

An outstanding feature is the Lockheed hydraulic braking system, with 2 leading shoes in front and a large friction area. The brakes require only light pedal pressure and will bring the car to a halt without grab or side-pull; they show no sign of fade under punishing conditions. The fly-off type handbrake, fitted between the seats, proved most effective on a steep gradient.

Engine

Some changes have been made to the engine, among which is the fitting of 1½in. S.U. carburettors with Vokes-type air cleaners. I found that these cleaners did not provide sufficient damping of carburettor roar.

There is a step-up in general performance—particularly at the bottom end of the scale, where acceleration is quite lively. Using 46 b.h.p., the engine can be worked hard without any sign of stress; it will run up to 6000 r.p.m. without fuss. During acceleration runs the motor remained quite smooth right up to peak r.p.m.

Maximum speed is reached on a reasonably short run, during which the engine seems quite at ease. With an 8 to 1 compression ratio, some pinking is noticeable and a higher grade fuel than the one at present available is desirable.

Our top-speed figure is the result of four runs over the measured quarter-mile, with accurate timing. A figure of 88.2 m.p.h. is a fine effort on low-octane fuel. Comfortable cruising speeds—road conditions permitting—are 60 to 70 m.p.h.

Gears and Transmission

Mounted centrally on the transmission tunnel, the gear-change lever is where it should be. The short lever, which is comfortably placed for the driver's left hand, is a pleasure to operate; travel is short, selection of gears positive. Gear ratios are perfectly balanced: the box is very silent in operation. Used harshly, the synchromesh can be over-ridden. The clutch requires a light pedal pressure only and does not shudder or slip.

Body and Fittings

Extremely well finished, the body is mounted on a robust box-section full chassis. The seats are upholstered in real leather and are of the individual bucket style. Ample leg-room is provided for tall people. Floor controls are well spaced, and there is room to rest the left foot on the floor when it is not operating the clutch. I found the accelerator pedal a little awkward to use, however, on a long trip.

Made of a high-quality pre-shrunk material, the hood

TWIN S.U. CARBURETTORS and Vokes-type air cleaners are standard on the TF. Engine layout is compact, but accessibility for maintenance is good

stows away neatly. Side-curtains are housed flat behind the rear seats, and there is a well-fitting tonneau cover. Paintwork and chromium plating are faultless throughout.

An entirely new recessed instrument panel is provided, with a handy-sized open glovebox on each side. Instruments, with white figures on black dials, include a large speedometer with trip and full mileage recorders and an inset clock. The rev counter is on the right and can be read at a glance. A central dial carries the ammeter and the oil-pressure and water-temperature gauges. A warning light instead of a fuel gauge must come in for criticism, since it is not in keeping with the remaining standard of the instrument panel.

Mounted on top of the facia, the rear-vision mirror gives a clear view, is quite stable, and does not at any time vibrate. The instruments are well illuminated for night driving, and a handy map-reading light is provided. Controls for headlights, clock, twin electric windscreen wipers, panel and map-reading lights, ignition and starter are below and beside the dials. A solenoid press-starter would be a distinct advantage and more in keeping with the rest of the car.

In all I found the MG a sheer delight to drive. It handles perfectly, offers a lively performance, and inspires confidence and safety. And it gives you comfort in good or bad weather, and in varied road conditions.

MODERN MOTOR — July 1954

ALL-AUSTRALIAN

SPORTLIGHT FEATURE

MG SPECIAL

SIDE VIEW of the rear-engined streamliner with designer Gordon Stewart at the wheel (above). He sits between the two petrol tanks.

REAR is smartly tapered to wasp-like tail. with twin exhaust pipes in place of the sting.

SLEEK, low, and fast, Les Wheeler's new rear-engined MG Special will soon be ready for trials—but it won't race until next Easter at the earliest.

Wheeler, a Parramatta (N.S.W.) chemist, doesn't believe in going off half-cocked. Before pitting this pale blue speedster against a bunch of tough rivals, he wants to be sure the car is ready to do its best—and that means 135 m.p.h., unblown, according to its designers.

Waiting a few more months will make little difference: two years of hard work have already gone into the car's design and construction, and no expense has been spared.

Blakehurst engineer Gordon Stewart worked together with Geoff Surtees in designing the car; in the early stages they enlisted the help of aircraft engineer Bert Hebron. After body lines had been worked out, the chassis was sent to Melbourne, where coachwork specialist Bob Baker made up the body from light aluminium alloy.

It's a magnificently finished job—and a unique feature of construction is the fact that one man can strip off all body panels in seven minutes flat. Except for two nuts on the nose-piece, the panels are held by aircraft-type Dzus fasteners, and the only tools needed for dismantling them are one screwdriver and one spanner.

ENGINE is that of Wheeler's old competition TC, with 12 to 1 compression ratio, twin carburettors. Run on methanol fuel, it develops 85 b.h.p.

ALL-AUSTRALIAN MG SPECIAL

The car's present power-plant is the overbored (1350 c.c.) engine from Wheeler's stripped TC, which won him many races at Mt. Druitt. With a compression ratio of 12:1 and twin carburettors, it is expected to churn out 85 b.h.p. at 6500 r.p.m., may even rev up to 7000.

If this engine fails to drive the car at 135 m.p.h. without supercharging, it will probably be replaced; in any event, a blower may be tried later. As a matter of interest, top speeds recorded here so far with engines of similar type are 111 m.p.h., unblown, 115 m.ph. with a supercharger.

In the face of this, expecting to reach 135 m.p.h. without a supercharger may sound optimistic; but then, no one connected with the car claims this is certain to be achieved—it is merely a goal they've set themselves, and towards which they are working.

Stewart and Wheeler will also experiment with tyres and wheels of different sizes, until they strike the right combination. At present the car rides on Austin-Healey wheels.

The gearbox is a standard MG TC job, with a shortened lever; the drive shaft arrangement is built up from R type MG drawings. Clutch and footbrake are hydraulically controlled, with direct-coupled Girling type master cylinders.

A Mercedes type de Dion rear end is fitted, with the movable joint in the centre; bars are Panhard pattern. Front suspension combines Morris Minor torsion bars with Y type MG shock-absorbers, and specially made connecting links. The Cooper steering-box and tie-rods are of the Morris Minor pattern; brakes are standard MG TC.

The interconnected twin petrol tanks, mounted each side of the cockpit and forming part of the body sides, will hold 25 gallons between them. Methanol fuel will be used; the car will do 14 m.p.g. in its present state, or about 8 m.p.g. with a blower.

Specially built to fit into the streamlined nose-piece, the radiator has the capacity of a normal TC. The engine sump holds 10¼ pints, and another three pints of oil are carried in the oil-cooler and pipes.

At present the engine gets cooling air only from a scoop under the body tray, but Bob Baker is going to put additional air intakes into the sides of the body, just behind each petrol tank. The handbrake, too, is yet to be fitted; it may go alongside the gear lever, or on the opposite side of the cockpit.

Car's dry weight is 10 cwt.; 149in. long overall, it has a 90in. wheelbase. Front track is 53in., rear 50in. It will race in the 1500 c.c. class.

When the Special is ready, Wheeler will start learning to drive all over again. Although he began racing four years ago, and was immediately successful, he hasn't raced for the past two years. Having decided to build a rear-engined racer, he realised that handling it would require an entirely different technique, and quit racing immediately, so as to be able to learn afresh, rather than have to fight deeply ingrained driving habits, acquired through long experience of front-engined cars.

The next Easter meeting at Bathurst will show whether Wheeler's two-year programme has been successful. If his car is as fast as it looks, he should have no trouble.

Expected to reach 135 m.p.h. with an unblown engine, this car has a unique body that one man can take apart in 7 minutes

FRONT is particularly striking; specially made grille preserves MG tradition.

COCKPIT fits driver snugly but does not cramp him; rear-vision mirrors are on the dash. Cut-down MG gear lever is at left; handbrake will go alongside it, or on the opposite side.

STRIPPED of body, car shows its sturdy chassis, de Dion type rear end.

MODERN MOTOR — January 1955

SHAPE of things to come — prototype of the first production MG to be fully streamlined.

MG PRODUCTION RACER

Le Mans was a tryout for prototype of future models

A NEW, more streamlined kind of MG may be introduced to the sports-car market next year.

Nuffields, the makers, entered a team of their latest experimental models at Le Mans—sleeker and more powerful than the old cars; from them the next production MG's will probably be designed.

It was the first team appearance of MG's at a race meeting in 20 years or so, but Nuffields were careful to point out that they weren't after the 1½-litre title: they were just using the event as a testing-ground for their prototypes.

The cars ran well, holding their own with some other well-known makes. Observers noted that their engines were easily the quietest on the course.

Afterwards the MG people seemed very happy about their showing, but pointed out that a lot more tests and refinements were needed.

They added that if the car continued to please them, the next MG production models would have a lot in common with the prototypes. And they would sell at a "very competitive price."

It's not likely, however, that anything will be heard about the production jobs until next year.

Nuffields admitted that body styles which caused high wind resistance had previously prevented speeds much in excess of 85 m.p.h.

It was with this knowledge in mind that a new aluminium, detachable two-seater body style was developed. It follows the general trend set by other sports-racers — a trend imposed by the aerodynamical requirements of high-speed cars.

Through the snubbed and curved (but still recognisable) MG grille air flows over the radiator and engine, then escapes through vents in the top of the bonnet.

A full-length undertray cuts wind resistance underneath; because this prevents circulation around the sump, an oil-cooler is fitted.

MG technicians quote a top speed of 115 m.p.h. from the prototypes.

The engine is a development of the B.M.C. "B" series unit, used in the MG Magnette and in some Austin and Morris models.

For Le Mans, an ingenious cylinder-head was fitted, giving 9.4 to 1 compression and a possible 82 b.h.p. at 5500 r.p.m.

(Continued on page 109)

GRILLE looks familiar, if nothing else does. Inset spotlamp, trapdoor bonnet, neatly faired taillights are other features of new full-width body.

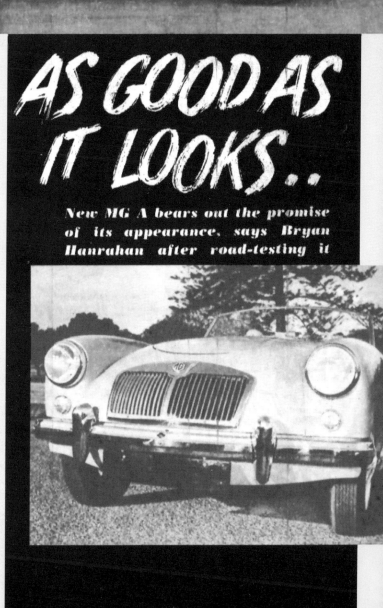

AS GOOD AS IT LOOKS..

New MG A bears out the promise of its appearance, says Bryan Hanrahan after road-testing it

THE Americans may not be able to build sports cars, but they have an unerring eye and those beckoning dollars for good British and Continental mounts.

So now more than half the production of the new MG A is being shipped from England straight across the Atlantic.

That means we don't get many at all—but it does not explain the shrinking violet tendencies of British Motors Corporation and the big MG distributors out here when it comes to the matter of a road test.

The A is a grand little car, and without going into the history of the MG breed, it certainly justifies the renowned "Safety First" slogan more than any of its predecessors have done.

Notwithstanding, this road test had to be done in a not quite run-in privately-owned vehicle. If the figures are a fraction behind what they should be, company interests and my nervous right foot under the eye of the owner are to blame.

With this reservation, I am satisfied that the data here gives a pretty accurate picture of this little beauty's performance.

A Preamble

If you are going to read this road test with the idea of getting some value out of it, a little exercise in perspective is necessary.

Don't compare the car's performance with either the Triumph or the Austin-Healey. Engine capacity is half-a-litre down on the Triumph and a full litre less than the Austin—and the price of the standard MG (£1256) gives away £200 to £300 to either of its bigger rivals.

On the road the MG has a personality all its delightful own. Breeding is the reason for this. Years of experience with small sports models

MODERN MOTOR — July 1956

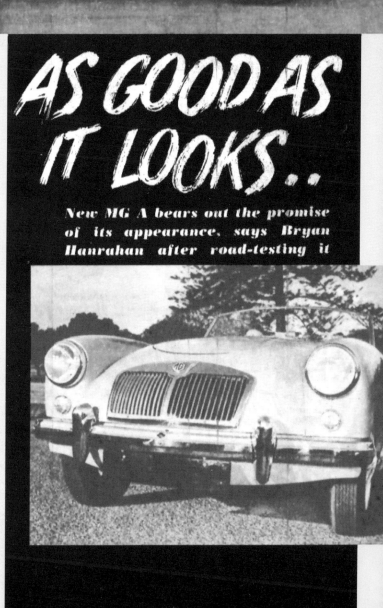

104 MARQUE SPOTLIGHT SERIES

TAIL, tenacious on curves, responds instantly to the steering-wheel.

SEATS give excellent support, controls fall readily to hand, arm-rest on transmission tunnel adds extra comfort—but speedo, at extreme right, can't be seen by passenger. BELOW: Engine is readily accessible; so is the brake-and-clutch master cylinder (top left).

and record-breakers have gone into the design.

Prototypes first appeared in public at Le Mans in 1955. This was part of an extensive proving programme which embraced high-speed running at Montlhery, on the Nurburgring and in the Alps. Only recently production models scored well in their class in the Mille Miglia.

In standard trim it is not a true 100 m.p.h. car—95.8 was my flying quarter-mile speed—although only slightly favorable conditions will bring up the century.

However, special tuning data and equipment is available from the manufacturer, and I would imagine the car could be worked up to 105 m.p.h. or so with very little trouble.

Acceleration, as one would expect again, falls off rather markedly after 80 m.p.h. (My word, what we demand from 1½-litres these days!)

On the Road

I slid into the driving seat and made my first acquaintance with the MG at 6 o'clock on a cold, windy morning.

After the first couple of miles I knew it was something specially good. There was never any hesitation in putting one's hand on to the necessary control—they happen to be placed just right. This is what I mean by breeding.

The seat is small, but gives excellent support. It is upholstered in leather—a minor but reassuring point.

Some five inches of gear lever sends instant and clear messages to the four-speed box through near-unbeatable synchromesh.

The engine had warmed by this time, and a couple of powerful headlights (it was still dark) urged the car along.

The first bend, well illuminated by the beam spread, came up. Brakes, gears and throttle worked together in inspiring harmony, and the car seemed to settle down even more firmly on the road as it went around.

Yes, it had to be steered. But no conscious effort was needed to do so, which is the highest tribute I can pay the rack-and-pinion mechanism, endowed with spot-on precision, directness and light action.

On the next corner I gently abused her. Dropping a cog too low, I trod on the acceleration as I entered. We proceeded broadside for a few feet, front and rear end balanced perfectly by that marvellous steering until the wheels gripped on a better patch of road.

Composed and orderly, the MG made off like a dart.

Needless to say, I had forgotten the owner in the first few exciting minutes at the wheel. He didn't seem to mind, though. He was good enough to allow a really thorough test to be carried out.

She was running so smoothly and

sweetly that I had to make a deliberate mental check of her qualities.

Nothing so far invited criticism except a small reflection in the curved screen. The hood was up, but I could see clearly in all important directions.

Speed and Brake Tests

At the test strip I consulted the rev counter as I ran the engine up to its useful maximum of just over 5000 r.p.m. in the intermediate gears in readiness for the first timed standing quarter.

Six runs were made in all. After four we checked the times—identical.

One would have expected a progressive improvement as the familiarisation process went on—but no. This MG had befriended me; there was no need to court her affections or allow for cranky ways.

So, the standing quarter stood at 19.9 seconds, and the watches returned a mean 95.8 m.p.h. for the flying quarter-mile.

Into the acceleration runs—0-50 in 9.9 sec. Not a trace of clutch slip, but wheelspin had to be watched.

Zero to 60, to 70, to 80 m.p.h.; that sweet little engine hammered out each figure four times.

Was it upset? Not a bit of it. The same remarkable consistency throughout.

The idling note never changed, and when switched off the engine died immediately: no fumes, no smells, no variation on the water temperature gauge.

The brakes had been punished on the acceleration runs to heat them up, so we immediately did the 30 m.p.h. to a stop—32 feet 3 inches on damp bitumen!

HOOD has generous rear window, fits well, and doesn't let in the weather; but, like most sports cars, MG A looks better without it.

CORD in top of door recess releases the latch—there are no external door handles. Behind panel, it can't be worked accidentally.

MAIN SPECIFICATIONS — MGA

ENGINE: 4 cylinder o.h.v.; bore 3.025mm; stroke 89mm; capacity 1489 c.c.; compression ratio, 8.15 to 1; rate h.p., 13.2, developed 68 at 5500 r.p.m.; twin SU semi–downdraught carburettors, electric fuel pump, 12-v coil ignition

TRANSMISSION: 4 speed gearbox, floor lever, synchromesh on top three, single dry–plate clutch; hpoid bevel final drive, 4.3 to 1 ratio

CHASSIS: Separate, box section.

SUSPENSION: Coil and wishbones in front, semi elliptic at rear, telescopic hydraulic shock absorbers.

BRAKES: 10in hydraulics, 2 leading shoes front; lining area, 134.4 sq. in.

STEERING: Rack and pinion, 2 2.3 turns lock–to–lock, 28ft. turning circle.

DIMENSIONS: Wheelbase 7ft. 10in.; truck, front 3ft. 11½in., rear 4ft. 0¾in., length 13ft., width 4ft. 10in., height 4ft. 2in.; ground clearance, 6in.; weight, 17cwt. unladen.

FUEL TANK: 10 gallons.

PERFORMANCE ON TEST

CONDITIONS: Cold, wet, damp bitumen, longitudinal breeze, two occupants, premimum fuel.

MAXIMUM SPEED: 97 m.p.h.

FLYING quarter mile: 95.8 m.p.h.

STANDING quarter mile: 19.9 sec.

MAXIMUM SPEEDS in gears: First, 27 m.p.h.; second, 44; third, 68; top, 97.

ACCELERATION from rest through gears: 0-30, 3.9sec.; 0-40, 6sec.; 0-50, 9.9sec.; 0-60, 12.6sec.; 0-70, 18.9sec.; 0-80, 24.8sec.

ACCELERATION in top and third gears (third in brackets): 10-30, 10.9 sec. (7); 20-40, 10.4sec. (5.2); 30-50, 10.6sec. (7); 40-60, 11.2sec. (8); 50-70, 12.8sec. (—); 60-80, 16 sec. (—).

BRAKING: 32ft. 3in. to stop from 30 m.p.h.

PETROL CONSUMPTION: 42 m.p.g. at 30 m.p.h.; 33 at 60; 36 m.p.g. overall.

SPEEDOMETER: Accurate at 30 m.p.h.; 3 percent fast at 60, 5 percent fast at 90.

PRICE: £1256 including tax

Nor did they at any time lose their smooth power, or cause the car to deviate off course.

We confirmed them with a 40-mile run through the hills, which was an exhilarating experience.

Pause for mental digging.

NOISE.—Engine extremely quiet, exhaust very fruity under load, wind not obtrusive up to almost 80 m.p.h.

HOOD.—Slight flapping on occasions, but not a drop of water inside and no draughts unless hand-signalling. Better stowed and erected by two people.

COMFORT.—Like being in bed.

WIPERS.—Cleared lots of screen. but two speeds would be welcome.

SMALL CONTROLS.—Horn push in traditional place on dash—not the best spot. Flashing indicator control on the dash, too.

SERIOUS FAULT. — Speedometer on right where passenger cannot see

(Continued on page 109)

NEW TWIN-CAM M.G.

TWIN O.H.C. engine churns out 108 b.h.p.

"Safety Faster" is the motto for this disc-braked 120 m.p.h. version of the MG A, says Harold Dvoretsky after driving it

I'VE just driven the new twin-overhead-camshaft MG A — and, brother, can this little beast go!

The Twin-Cam (that's its official name) was announced in England on July 15, and the day before B.M.C. invited a batch of us motoring pen-pushers to sample it on the Fighting Vehicle Research Establishment's test track at Chobham, a few miles to the south-west of London.

Six of the new jobs were waiting there for us. Apart from the Dunlop centre-lock disc wheels, and the name Twin-Cam, spelt out in chromed letters alongside the scuttle air-exit grilles and on the boot-lid, they didn't look any different from the normal MG A.

The main difference, of course, was under the bonnet.

The New Engine

Here sits the new twin o.h.c version of the B Series B.M.C. engine, bored out to a capacity of 1589 c.c. Working on 9.9 to 1 compression, it churns out 97 b.h.p. at 5000 revs, rising to 108 at 6700.

The camshafts are driven by duplex roller chain from a half-speed shaft, gear-driven from the crankshaft. Twin semi-downdraught SU's take care of the carburation, and petrol is supplied by an electric SU pump housed in the boot. A finned cast-aluminium sump helps the cooling.

B.M.C. quote 7000 revs as safe

FULL HOUSE in the engine-room—but main tuning components are easily accessible. Rocker covers are polished aluminium. RIGHT: Dunlop disc brakes on all wheels are the other big feature. Of caliper type, they allow quick pad changes, are extremely efficient and impervious to fade.

SPECIFICATIONS

ENGINE: 4-cylinder, twin o.h.c.; bore 75.4mm., stroke 88.9mm., capacity 1589 c.c.; compression ratio 9.9 to 1; maximum b.h.p. 108 at 6700 r.p.m.; twin SU semi-downdraught carburettors; SU electric fuel pump, 12v. ignition.

TRANSMISSION: Single dry-plate clutch, 8in. diameter; four-speed gearbox synchromeshed on top three; ratios—1st 15.652, 2nd 9.520, 3rd 5.908, top 4.3 to 1; reverse 20.468 to 1; hypoid bevel final drive, 4.3 to 1 ratio.

SUSPENSION: Front independent, by coil springs and wishbones; semi-elliptics at rear; hydraulic shock-absorbers all round.

STEERING: Rack - a n d - pinion.

WHEELS: Centre-lock discs, with 5.90 by 15in. Roadspeed tyres.

BRAKES: Dunlop caliper-type disc brakes, hydraulically operated; mechanical handbrake working on rear discs.

CONSTRUCTION: Box - section chassis, braced for torsional rigidity.

FUEL TANK: 10 gallons.

engine speed and claim a top speed of "around 120 m.p.h." with the standard 4.3 to 1 MG A rear axle.

Recommending 6500 revs as gearchange point, they say the Twin-Cam will reach 100 m.p.h. from rest in 31 seconds, and 110 in 38 seconds.

Twin cams were first tried on an MG A which raced in the 1955 Dundrod T.T. A later, supercharged version of this engine powered the experimental M G EX181 streamliner in which Stirling Moss reached 245 m.p.h. and smashed a string of records on the Utah Salt Flats a year ago.

So there's a lot of sound developmental work behind the new donk.

Disc Brakes, Too

The other big difference on the Twin-Cam model is Dunlop disc brakes on all four wheels.

Of caliper type, they allow quick pad changes. Their stopping power is fantastic, and no amount of hard work can cause them to fade.

The centre-lock wheels are dished to accommodate the brakes, and ventilated to assist cooling. Enthusiasts may wail at the disappearance of wire wheels — but B.M.C. claim that the superior efficiency of disc brakes makes the extra ventilation provided by the wire wheel unnecessary.

They warn that the disc brakes will not be available on the standard MG A, which will continue to be produced in its present form; nor will it be possible to convert standard MG's to the twin-cam engine, as this would require too many engineering modifications.

Now that I've told you all about the new car's features, let's get on with the testing.

On the Track

The Chobham testing-ground includes a twisty, slightly banked two-mile circuit, and we belted those six Twin-Cams around it with a will.

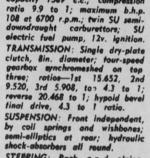

The new engine seems no noisier than the normal 1½-litre job, but it certainly packs a lot more power. It's oh-so-easy to spin the wheels on dry tarmac in a first-gear take-off!

It took me a couple of laps to get used to the course and the extra power of this MG. After that I went out to try for "the ton" which, on a short circuit like this one, required a bit of jiggery-pokery.

I'm afraid "the ton" avoided me; all I could get was 98 m.p.h. on a half-mile straight entered from a lowly banked tight curve. For my money that wasn't bad.

NEW TWIN-CAM MG A

I lapped the track in absolute comfort, with little worry of control, in 1 minute 43 seconds — but two brighter sparks did get around in 1 minute 30, which is really motoring on that circuit.

This new MG has all the virtues of the standard car. It's never vicious; there's plenty of warning of intended rear-wheel breakaway, and correction — provided it's taken right away — is an easy matter.

I managed only one through-the-gears timed start. This was for the 0-80 m.p.h. bracket, and she did it in 20.8 seconds. I'm not prepared to swear by that one — but I'm ready to believe those factory claims of 0-100 in 31 seconds and 0-110 in 38.

A few weeks ago I tried out a Standard MG A hardtop, just for comparison. In that car 80 m.p.h. came up in 31 seconds.

Trying the Brakes

After a few high-speed runs I turned my attention to the new disc brakes. They're wonderful — there's no other word for it. The way they bring the car to a stop from 90 m.p.h. is a revelation.

Applying the brakes with a firm but not heavy pedal pressure, you feel them pulling up strongly and then wait for the usual drum-brake fade; with the discs, of course, it never comes, and you come to a full stop with nary a falter.

My lap averages were improving all the time, and had I done the high-speed brake tests first, I might have managed "the ton" and a faster circuit time.

All in all, this is a delightful car, and I can hardly wait to get it out on the road for a full test.

A suggestion to B.M.C. — why not amend the MG slogan for the Twin-Cam from "Safety Fast" to "Safety Faster"?

Range and Extras

The Twin-Cam will be available in both roadster and coupe form, and buyers will be offered a wide range of comfort and competition extras such as a low plastic windscreen, body-gripping luxury seats, etc.

It will not replace the standard MG A models, which continue unchanged. Pricewise, there's a big difference. The Twin-Cam will cost £180stg. basic more than the standard MG, which should mean a jump of about £375 in Australia by the time freight, duty and sales tax are added — say £1750 Aust. for the Twin-Cam roadster.

But don't expect the new cars "down under" for quite a while. Preliminary orders for the Twin-Cam from U.S.A. and Canada alone will account for the first seven months' production. Unless output is bumped up considerably, you won't see the Twin-Cam until late next year. ● ●

(Continued from page 103)

MG PROTOTYPE

Bore is 73.025 mm., stroke 89 mm., capacity 1489 c.c. The overhead valves are operated by pushrods, and there are three main bearings on the crankshaft.

Most important feature of the engine is the fuel induction system. Fed into the inlet ports by two S.U. carburettors, the fuel passes straight through the head into a balance tube, whence it is drawn by cylinder suction to provide perfectly equal distribution.

Gear and rear-end ratios correspond to 47 m.p.h. in first, 71 in second, 91 in third, and 115 in top. Gear-change is by a short, centrally mounted remote-control lever.

The chassis used in the prototype was introduced in the streamlined single-seater which broke records at over 150 m.p.h. on the Utah salt lakes (U.S.A.) in August last year.

It has a sturdy box-section frame designed to combine strength with ability to carry a comfortable body, and to retain its strength through the bashing which sports cars so often receive.

Narrow in front, to give a lively steering lock, the frame widens out behind the front wheels, where it is reinforced with a special welded section which goes through at scuttle height and crosses beneath the transmission line.

The frame narrows again to accommodate the rear wheels, and rises to give the rear axle room to move. The chassis is strongly reinforced at all stress points.

Front suspension is of the coil type proved in the TD and TF series, with wishbones of unequal length mounted on top to the arms of Armstrong hydraulic dampers.

At the rear, semi-elliptics which lie almost parallel to the road (no forward inclination for roll understeer being considered necessary) are attached at the back by shackles, and by normal fixed anchorage at the forward end.

Low in the frame, ahead of the rear axle, are the 12-volt battery and the dual S.U. electrical fuel pump, drawing from a 20-gallon tank. Above the tank is the spare wheel. A smaller tank would be used on production models, allowing more luggage space.

Dimensions are: length, 150 in.; width, 58 in.; height, 41 in.; wheelbase, 94 in.; track (front), 47⅞ in.; (rear), 48¼ in. ● ● ●

(Continued from page 106)

MG A TEST

it (unnoticed earlier because separate corrected speedo in use). Very silly mistake in a car which will be used a lot in competition work. All dials legible, though.

Through the hills the car was sure-footed as a cat. The tail, tenacious on curves, responds instantly to the steering wheel. Rough and loose going were handled ably by the suspension. Roll kept well in check. Firmish ride at low speeds. Good at speed over bumpy patches. Wise to remember ground clearance six inches.

Gearbox, steering and suspension combined to make the run sheer delight. Cornering powers are high even for a sporting mount. Third in the close ratios will take you up to 68 m.p.h.

On the way back we cruised quite happily at 80 m.p.h. Petrol worked out overall to 36 m.p.g.

Down to Details

But I picked one lovers' quarrel with the car when I went over it in daylight; the finish isn't quite what we have come to expect on MG's. Possibly the A's get churned out a little too fast, in view of the great demand for them.

When I say the trim is untidy, I mean by accepted MG standards—it would still do credit to many cars.

But the paint was not the best, and there is a hideous line of rivets low down on each side of the car.

The only spectacular thing about the engine is its performance. In design it is a straightforward o.h.v. four, inclined to reveal its numerical character only in low speeds.

Engine compartment, under a forward-opening bonnet, is well filled. Most regular maintenance points are not, however, difficult to get at.

Besides a reasonable boot by sporting standards there are useful door pockets and a glove locker, but no room behind the seats.

Standard wheels are pressed steel, bolted on. Knock-off wire wheels are extra. So, too, is a telescopic wheel column—but I think that, whatever your size and shape, a comfortable driving position can be found with the fixed wheel.

Detail equipment generally is generous; self-parking wipers; variable-intensity instrument lighting and fly-off handbrake—very efficient, too.

Independent front end is on coil springs, semi-elliptics at rear.

All in all, the "A" is a grand machine, in the best MG tradition.

"First of a new line," the manufacturers say. Let's hope it's a long one; and that import restrictions and a fine British product do not, paradoxically, continue for long to make one wish he was American. ● ● ●

First Australian road test of the new MG A Twin-Cam shows it's the first production MG that can genuinely exceed 100 m.p.h., reports Bryan Hanrahan

TWO CAMS TURNING

ONCE again you can thank Melbourne racing driver and Morris agent Peter Manton for a road test of the latest — and fastest — car of its name in Australia.

Not that he was very happy, mind you, to see his Twin-Cam MG A move off for the day . . . all £1867/5/1 worth of it. Would YOU be, if it was yours?

I'll bet you wouldn't — neither is the mighty BMC organisation, nor even the Victorian distributors, prepared to run one in for road-testing.

Why should they, when Peter is prepared to be the fall guy? They get their road test anyway, don't they?

About the Car

Now, about this Twin-Cam. I won't go into the general details of the car, since it's basically the now familiar MG A — so let's get straight on to the things that are different about it.

These are: the twin-overhead-camshaft layout of the four-cylinder, 1589 c.c. engine, the centre-lock ventilated disc wheels, the tiny "Twin-Cam" nameplate on the bonnet, the caliper-type disc brakes on all wheels—and a performance that's well worth experiencing.

The car also has better seats, trim and general finish, presumably because it's fully imported.

Power output is quoted as 108 b.h.p. at 6700 r.p.m., on a compression ratio of 9.9 to 1. The rev-counter is red-banded between 6500 and the 7500 top calibration; safe rev limit is said to be 7000.

Its Performance

The makers also claim the Twin-Cam will go from rest to 100 m.p.h. in 31 seconds and to 110 m.p.h. in 38; and they quote its tops speed at "between 110 and 120 m.p.h."

There's a fair bit of latitude in the top-speed claim, so I assume the same latitude in the acceleration figures—mine were nothing like so good.

Apart from the pleasure, etc., of David McKay's company, I wish he'd been over in Melbourne so that I could have helped HIM do the test.

This is the skeleton of what I got: 0-100 m.p.h. — 38.1sec.

MODERN MOTOR — August 1959

SECRET of latest MG's 108 m.p.h. performance is the new 1589 c.c., twin o.h.c. engine with 9.9 to 1 compression. Disc brakes all round, too!

MAIN SPECIFICATIONS

ENGINE: 4-cylinder, twin o.h.c.; bore 75.4mm., stroke 88.9mm., capacity 1589 c.c.; compression ratio 9.9 to 1; maximum b.h.p 108 at 6700 r.p.m.; twin semi-downdraught carbs. SU electric fuel pump; 12v. ignition.
TRANSMISSION: Single dry-plate clutch; 4-speed gearbox synchromeshed on top 3 gears; ratios, 1st 15.652, 2nd 9.520, 3rd 5.908, top 4.3, reverse 20.468 to 1; hypoid bevel final drive, 4.3 to 1 ratio.
SUSPENSION: Front independent, by coils and wishbones; semi-elliptics at rear; telescopic shockers all round.
STEERING: Rack-and-pinion; 3¼

turns lock-to-lock; 34ft. 3in. turning circle.
WHEELS: Centre-lock discs, with 5.90 by 15in. Roadspeed tyres.
BRAKES: Dunlop hydraulic caliper-type disc brakes on all wheels; mechanical handbrake on rear discs.
CONSTRUCTION: Box - section chassis, braced for torsional rigidity.
DIMENSIONS: Wheelbase 7ft. 10in.; track, front 3ft. 11½in., rear 4ft. 0¾in.; length 13ft., width 4ft. 10in., height 4ft. 2in., ground clearance 6in.
WEIGHT as tested: 21¼cwt.; unladen, 17½cwt.
FUEL TANK: 10 gallons.

PERFORMANCE ON TEST

CONDITIONS: Cool, gusty cross-wind; damp bitumen, two occupants; premium fuel with 40 percent benzol.
BEST SPEED: 108 m.p.h.
FLYING quarter-mile: 106.8 m.p.h.
STANDING quarter-mile: 18.4s.
MAXIMUM in indirect gears (to 6500 r.p.m.): 1st, 42 m.p.h.; 2nd, 65; 3rd, 96.
ACCELERATION from rest through gears: 0-30, 3.9s.; 0-40, 5.9s.; 0-50, 9.7s.; 0-60, 12.6s.; 0-70, 18.6s.; 0-80, 24.3s.; 0-90, 31.0s.; 0-100, 38.1s.

ACCELERATION in top (with third in brackets): 30-50, 8.2s. (5.1); 40-60, 8.0s. (4.9); 50-70, 8.0s. (5.2); 60-80, 8.9s. (6.1); 70-90, 10.0s. (8.1); 80, 100, 10.2s.
BRAKING: 30ft. 2in. to stop from 30 m.p.h. in neutral; 159ft. 3in. to stop from 90 m.p.h. in top gear. Tapley meter reading 98 percent.
FUEL CONSUMPTION: 44.2 m.p.g. at constant 30 m.p.h.; 26 at 60; 17.5 overall for 92-mile test.
SPEEDOMETER: 2 m.p.h. fast at 30 m.p.h.; 6 m.p.h. fast at 90.

PRICE: £1867 including tax

Top speed — 106.8 m.p.h.
Best speed — 108 m.p.h.
BUT . . . there are a few factors to take into account:
● The weather and the road were dampish — which is all right for the motor, but not so good for wheel adhesion. Best I could do for a clean getaway was to drop in the clutch at 2000 r.p.m. Rev minimum desirable for a good take-off is 2500 r.p.m.; the torque doesn't really get active till then.
● The run-up on the most suitable test track I could find was limited to two miles, and a certain allowance had to be made for milk trucks when rounding a slight curve. Under the circumstances, my best run of 108 m.p.h. wasn't at all bad.
● The fuel — about 40 percent benzol and premium — and the state of tune. Peter is naturally still experimenting with both.
● The complete difference in character between Peter's Twin-Cam and the first models that were reported on by the British motoring Press when this latest MG was announced a year ago. These reports said the car was

very rough-running at low revs and had to have the firm finesse of handling that a sports-racing car needs.

Now, Peter's car has a split personality. Below 2500 revs it's rather like driving an automatic with two halves of an over-ripe grapefruit acting as the torque-converter—it's slow, but so SMOOTH. About 2500 r.p.m. things are faster than a game of Russian roulette with every chamber loaded. I think the car may have had some production modifications which may have affected claimed performance.

● Lastly, it's a friend's car—I didn't go over 6500 revs in the indirect gears, and sometimes I balked at that when the noise got too much for my conscience.

Think on these things, and above all remember that the Twin-Cam is not just a 1936 Chev that will run on kero and can be tuned with a pair of quick-grips and a hairpin.

She's in a class where all the females are EXPECTED to be temperamental.

Anyway, if you listened to that engine pitching into things around 6500 revs, you'd realise that it is a very busy piece of machinery indeed. It makes not so much a loud but a very, very BUSY noise.

Nothing came through the sump, I'm glad to say. But the water temperature hopped up and down a bit on the acceleration runs—never near the danger mark, though.

But for two points, I am reasonably happy with the speed and acceleration runs, all things considered.

One thing I didn't like was the amount of heat that comes off the engine (tests were done with hood and side-screens up for maximum streamline effect). Same thing happens at sustained high cruising speeds. It was quite a cold day—I boil to

COCKPIT changes from normal MG A include a fully leather-covered dash, comfier seats. General finish is better (car is fully imported).

think of summer motoring in a Twin-Cam, even with hood down.

The other was the effect of the gusty cross-wind on the car at 70 m.p.h. and beyond. The whole car would move sideways.

Which brings us to handling.

Handling and Braking

This is not the MG of tradition—a perky, brisk little runabout beloved, alas, by the type who really appreciates legs more than wheels.

It's a serious high-performance motor-car.

Beware, unless you're an experienced, serious driver. You can so easily get into trouble.

I'm in no way criticising the Twin-Cam's handling; it's first class. But

underneath the throttle pedal is a piece of dynamite that could go off at the wrong time on a corner.

If it happened to you—you alone would be to blame.

The steering is almost as good as you can get; the Dunlop disc brakes on all four wheels are better than anything imagined a few years back—no fade, no pulling aside, very little effort at the pedal.

They are caliper-type, self-cleaning, self-drying, and self-adjusting. It takes about two minutes per wheel to change pads.

The 159ft. 3in. stopping distance from 90 m.p.h. quoted in the performance panel was as uneventful as stopping from 20 m.p.h. at traffic lights.

Other Points

Just to sit in Peter's car is to love it. The seats are much more comfortable than the buckets fitted to the MG A's part-assembled in Australia. The finish and carpets are better. The dash is covered with semi-matt leather cloth instead of highly reflective duco.

And, praise be, that nasty, rattling, sticking, clicking trafficator switch, of which you never know whether it's on or off or really on the blink on the standard MG A,, is replaced by something that bears no resemblance to it—and WORKS.

Finally, don't take the fuel figure of 17.5 m.p.g. seriously. The test was much too short and swift for it to be anything like normal expectations. And please note that the performance panel gives "theoretical" maximums in indirect gears at 6500 r.p.m. — fact is, I changed up whenever the engine got so busy I couldn't bear the thought of Peter's face if I came back with a conrod in my hand.

(Test car by courtesy of Peter Manton, Monaro Motors, Melbourne.)

MG SEEKS RECORDS

THE MG Car Company announced on April 15 that a streamlined MG Special is being built in England for a fresh attack on International Class F (1500 c.c.) records.

It is described as "an entirely new record car, embodying many advanced design features." Details are still secret, but photo at right shows an eighth-scale model of the streamliner.

Stirling Moss will drive the car, and the record attempts will take place on the Bonneville Salt Flats, Utah, in August.

Present world record for 1½-litre cars is 204.2 m.p.h. It was set by Lt.-Col. A. T. Goldie-Gardiner in MG record car EX 135 at Dessau, Germany, in 1939. The new car should beat this mark with ease: speeds "of the order of four miles per minute" are expected. ● ● ●

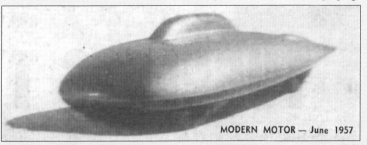

MODERN MOTOR — June 1957

MODEL of the new MG streamliner in which Stirling Moss will attack a series of Class F world records in August. Expected speed is 240 m.p.h.

"OUR JACK" with his latest creation—a real wolf in sheep's clothing (the MG-Climax, not J. Brabham).

Ex-champ has devised an engine swap that turns new MG Midget into a giant-killer, writes David Phipps after a private tryout

MG-CLIMAX FROM BRABHAM

JACK BRABHAM has done it again! First the Herald-Climax, now a Climax-engined Midget—and this time the results are even more amazing.

In bare figures, an 80 percent power boost improves acceleration from 0 to 50 m.p.h. by over 100 percent, halves the time required to go from 40 to 60 m.p.h. in top gear, and raises maximum speed by 25 m.p.h. On the road it turns a pleasant, good-handling but not particularly lively little roadster into a real high-performance sports car.

For all its implications, the Brabham conversion for the Midget is remarkably simple. It consists merely of replacing the standard engine and clutch with a 1216c.c. Coventry-Climax FWE unit and a special 7½-inch clutch. (Surprising as it may seem, the Climax engine is 40lb. lighter than the B.M.C. unit, with beneficial effects on weight distribution.) An 8000 r.p.m. tachometer is also supplied, and total price of the conversion, fitted, is £360stg.

The test car also had disc brakes on the front wheels and an anti-roll bar — both of which are recommended optional extras — and 5.60 by 13in. Dunlop B7 tyres, the latter mainly to ensure safety at speeds in excess of 100 m.p.h.

Naturally, the conversion is also applicable to the Midget's twin brother, the Austin-Healey Sprite, in both Mark I and Mark II form. In fact, the most obvious application of this conversion would seem to be a used Mark I Sprite, which could probably be obtained and converted at a total cost only £100 above that of a new Midget or Mark II Sprite.

The Climax FWE, a four-cylinder, single-overhead-camshaft unit, has a very good reputation following years of extremely successful racing. As fitted to the Midget, it produces 83 b.h.p. at 6400 revs, yet is even more flexible than the standard MG engine. It also compares very favorably in terms of fuel economy, starts easily from cold, warms up quickly and shows no sign of temperament in city traffic.

CLIMAX fits neatly in Midget's bay, is 40lb. lighter than normal unit but gives 80 percent more power. Theoretical maximum is 112 m.p.h.

On the Road

As can be imagined, with the free-revving Climax engine allied to the agility of the Midget, this is a most enjoyable car to drive — as I found when Jack lent me one for a tryout.

Seating position is good, and pedals, instruments and minor controls are all well placed. The test car's appearance was enhanced by the fitting of a three-spoke wood-rim steering-wheel. Even with the top up, visibility is quite good for a car of this type.

The great thing about the Climax-engined Midget is that it can take advantage of the smallest gaps to pass slow-moving traffic. All its responses are immediate: it goes where it is pointed, and it does so quickly. This applies even if top gear is used most of the time.

The keen driver is not likely to stay permanently in top, however, for the gearshift is very pleasant, and the standard gear ratios seem absolutely ideal for the Climax engine, giving maximum speeds (at 7000 r.p.m.) of 35 m.p.h. in first, 58 in second and 81 in third.

On paper, 7000 r.p.m. in top represents 112 m.p.h., which the car might reach under favorable conditions in hardtop form. The modified brakes are fully able to cope with the performance and seem immune to

fade in normal use. The lights are adequate for fast night driving — but the low build of the car causes some oncoming drivers to object to the dipped beams.

It says much for the basic Midget that the Climax-engined version will run straight and true at over 90 m.p.h. in very windy weather, and that the roadholding is in no way impaired by the much-increased power output.

Roadholding, in fact, is extremely good on smooth surfaces, and handling is almost up to sports/racing standards — thanks to the Midget's very precise steering and an anti-roll bar which virtually eliminates this model's characteristic roll over-steer.

On bumpy corners, however, the car tends to hop about somewhat and the ride is generally rather firm —as on all Midgets and Sprites. Brabham now plans to soften the rear springs — to improve both road-holding and ride — and also fit a Panhard rod.

Besides the disc brakes and an anti-roll bar, I would recommend fitting a hardtop as another essential adjunct for fast motoring. The standard soft top is extremely noisy at anything over 80 m.p.h. and also tends to lift away from the top of the windscreen at higher-than-standard speeds, but is prevented from blowing off by fasteners at each end of the screen. The exhaust note also becomes rather obtrusive at over 5000 r.p.m., although the Midget muffler is very effective at lower engine speeds.

Externally, the Midget-Climax is indistinguishable from a standard model. This feature, in conjunction with its ability to out-accelerate all mass-produced sports cars under 3 litres, will give it a special appeal for many people. And for anyone who wants a fast, small sports car with character, Jack's latest creation could well be the answer.

● ● ●

MEET the MG B: Straight-through styling, wind-up windows, bigger motor, lighter weight, more performance.

IT'S not often we get new MG models, and to get two within a few days of each other is really something. But it's happened: I've just driven the all-new MG B two-seater and a new, small front-wheel drive saloon, the MG 1100.

The MG B, released in Britain on September 20, has a 1800c.c. motor in a completely restyled body—much on the squarer lines of the MG Midget and latest Austin-Healey Sprite—and with body refinements such as wind-up windows.

Power output is a lusty 94 b.h.p.—four more than the MG A, which this car replaces—and with its lighter unitary body/chassis, the MG B will easily exceed 100 m.p.h.

The new saloon is virtually a de-luxe version of the radical Morris 1100, described last month. The MG version, released on October 2, has a twin-carburettor engine developing 55 b.h.p., traditional MG grille and different interior.

But first, the two-seater.

MG B Is All New

The MG B is frankly aimed at the U.S. market, where the ability to reach the magic "ton" is a powerful sales magnet.

Its predecessor, the MG A, began as a 1½-litre car and, during its production life of seven years, stretched its capacity to 1622c.c.

With its robust chassis frame and

A 100 m.p.h. two-seater and "hydrolastic" small saloon are outstanding newcomers to MG stable, reports Douglas Armstrong

sound construction, it well earned its marque tag of "Safety Fast," but its weight and relatively small engine made 100 m.p.h. difficult to attain.

There is no such difficulty with the "B." After driving the car, even in pouring rain, I can say that B.M.C.'s target of an "easy" hundred has been gained—plus.

By increasing the bore of the cur-

rent B.M.C. B-series engine, the capacity has been raised from 1622c.c. to 1798c.c. The bore size is enlarged from 72.2mm. to 80.26mm., the stroke remaining at 88.9.

It is not, however, just a "bored-out" block, but a specially-cast one with the same external dimensions as the standard B-series. The compression ratio is up from 8.3:1 to 8.75.

FROM tail, MG B looks like the smaller MG Midget or Austin-Healey Sprite. Panel layout (right) is functional; horn button is now on wheel.

TWO NEW MGs

Gross output is 94 b.h.p. at 5500 r.p.m., max. torque 107lb./ft. at 3500.

This new engine has really got some steam, without recourse to separate inlet and exhaust ports for each cylinder. B.M.C. have collected a great deal of data over the years on how to extract real power from simple siamesed-port, cast-iron heads.

The engine drives through a Borg and Beck single-plate dry clutch, with spring type diaphragm—new to MG.

The four-speed gearbox has the familiar remote-control lever, but does not yet have synchromesh on low gear. Overall ratios are: first, 14.21; 2nd, 8.65; 3rd, 5.36; top, 3.09; reverse, 18.58 to 1.

Top gear gives a road speed of 17.9 m.p.h. per 1000 r.p.m.

Suspension is virtually the same—coil springs at the front, leaf springs at the back.

Lockheed hydraulic braking is used, with discs at the front and drum brakes at the rear.

The petrol tank has a capacity of 10 gallons, and an oil-cooler is standard on export models.

Perhaps the most amazing thing about the new model is its rigidity: although of monocoque construction, this open car has as rigid a structure as the separate-chassis MG A.

I talked to Sid Enever, the engineer who has been the technical brain behind so many famous MGs, including the special record-breakers, and he told me that the "B's" unitary frame is as stiff in beam and torsion as the model's predecessor.

Certainly the MG B has that same taut, all-in-one-piece feeling.

The new body shape is most attractive to the eye. Its lines follow that of the smaller Midget, but have scalloped headlight treatment, rather like the Renault Floride, and a neat "traditional" radiator grille.

MG 1100: Based on the new hydrolastic-sprung Morris, small MG saloon is distinguished by upright grille and more lavish trim. Transverse engine has twin carbs, develops 55 b.h.p. against Morris's 50 (gross).

Interior Fittings

The interior trim (black leather and white piping on the car I drove) is most attractive. The well-equipped dashboard is leathercloth-covered, with a padded roll on the sill, and black "crackle" anti-reflection finish around the large rev-counter and 120 m.p.h. speedometer. The horn button is in the centre of the steering wheel —after all these years!

The car has the new B.M.C. black plastic door handles and winders. They look good, besides being less liable to cause injury in a crash.

The seats slide well back, will provide leg-room for drivers up to 6ft. 4in., and are nicely shaped for fast motoring. A shorter steering column would have been even better,

SCALLOPED nose gives MG B a Renault Floride look at the front. Hood tucks away neatly when not in use.

but it would probably have meant a redesigned dash. The customary MG gear lever is in the right place, and provides a quick, positive change. Pity there's no synchromesh on low.

Road view is splendid; even in pouring rain, with the Vynide hood erect, visibility through the three-piece rear window and side windows is good.

At the moment there is only an open two-seater in the catalogue; but with its curved windscreen, wind-up windows and swivelling quarter-lights, it is pretty obvious that there will soon be a fixed-head coupe.

There is reasonable space in the rear part of the cockpit for extra luggage or a child. MG give no capacity figures for the boot, but it provides reasonable space for a sporting car, despite the spare wheel.

Vivid Performance

The test car was still tight, but its performance was enough to convince me that this is the best "G" yet. Its ratios are well chosen and it reached 50 m.p.h. in second, 85 in third, and about 103 in top—and quickly. I would put its genuine maximum around 105-6 m.p.h.

The 1.8 motor has immense torque all the way up the range. There are no flat spots, either.

Such is the stability that I found myself driving at an indicated 100 m.p.h. on Birmingham's M5 Motorway in pouring rain, and on greasy surfaces. Through the curves the car would go at the ton as though on rails, and the disc-front/drum-rear braking set-up inspired the greatest confidence.

Ride is firm at low speeds, but improves at higher velocities.

With a combination of eager performance, ability to cruise at 90 and tremendous stability, the MG B is indeed an exciting car.

Basic price in Britain is £690, suggesting an Australian price around £1365, tax-paid. When you'll see the "B," though, I don't know. No definite plans for Australia have been made.

The great sales target at the moment is U.S.A. Ninety percent of the Abingdon factory's output of 1100 cars a week will go there.

MG 1100 Saloon

The new "family" MG is a mildly turned version of the fascinating Morris 1100. Although the fantastic ride, roadholding and cornering ability of the hydrolastic suspension are all there, I found myself no more impressed than with the wonderful little Morris.

Biggest changes are to the interior, where trim and comfort of the wide, deep seats are outstanding for a small car. The fascia is wood-pannelled.

The compression ratio, camshaft and basic east-west layout of the engine/transmission unit are identical to the Morris, but the extra carb is claimed to produce another 5 b.h.p.

Maximum speed is said to be in "the order of 85 m.p.h." I found that the test car would hold an indicated 80 on the motorway, but it took a downhill gradient to push it to 85—and then it dropped to a sustained 82 on the level.

It ran up to 65 in third; 0-50 (two-up) took 17 seconds.

Like the MG B, most MG 1100s are destined for the dollar-buyer. There are in two- and four-door versions, but no prices have been announced.

NEW 4-cylinder MG B engine develops 94 b.h.p. from 1798c.c., is more accessible for maintenance beneath wider bonnet than on MG A model.

New, chassisless MG B offers more engine, more comfort, but retains all the old zest, reports Bill Daly

GEE-WHIZ!

W HEN the late Jack Myers looked like being beaten by race handicappers, he would say "there's no substitute for inches", and forthwith bore the cylinders of his car our a fraction bigger.

Most of the time this formula worked successfully for Jack — just as it has for the just–released MG B.

Capable of 105 m.p.h. and offering every comfort for two people and their luggage, the latest version of this famous make has a bigger (1800c.c.) engine which, coupled with the car's new chassisless construction, makes it a delight to drive in town or country.

At 18½cwt., the B may be a little heavy for competition work — but it should certainly do better than the

NEW 1798c.c. engine develops 94 b.h.p. kicked test car to 105 m.p.h.

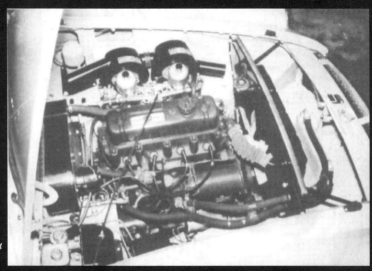

abortive twin-cam job of not so long ago. And it can accelerate this weight from rest to 90 m.p.h. in just over 32 seconds—or pull away smoothly from 15 m.p.h. in top gear.

The B's weightiness is justified by the provision of wide (36½in.) doors for easy entry, comfort-giving glass wind-up windows (just over two turns of the handle), a roomier cockpit with lots of elbow room, and all the leg-room adjustment any 6ft. 4in. midget might require.

Versatile Power-pack

Externally the new 1798c.c. engine appears unchanged—but it is, no doubt, the end of the line in the development of the 1½-litre B.M.C. unit, first produced in 1954 and progressively enlarged to 1588, then 1622c.c.

Bores have been enlarged once more, but there's no increase in stroke, although the casting has been altered internally to take the bigger bores; the inner wall of the tappet chest has been modified to retain adequate water passages.

Contact area between front and rear pairs of siamesed cylinders has been increased, and gudgeon-pin bosses now sport four holes instead of two, to give further internal cooling by oil spray. Crankshaft has been stiffened and main-bearing diameter increased by ⅛in. Minor head modifications round off the mechanical picture.

Under load, this enlarged, high-compression (8.8:1) version of the B series engine with twin SU carburettors has a much wider range of useful speeds than the B.M.C. touring vehicles, already renowned for smooth pulling power at low revs.

DASH (top right) is fully instrumented, gearshift a beauty. WELL behind seats (right) takes luggage or one small child. BOOT (below) loses much space to the spare wheel.

MAIN SPECIFICATIONS

ENGINE: 4-cylinder, o.h.v.; bore 80.26mm., stroke 88.9mm., capacity 1798c.c.; compression ratio 8.8:1; maximum b.h.p. 94 at 5500 r.p.m.; maximum torque 107lb./ft. at 3500; twin SU semi-downdraught carburettors, SU electric fuel pump; 12v. ignition.
TRANSMISSION: Single dry-plate clutch, hydraulically operated; 4-speed gearbox, synchromeshed on top three; overall ratios—1st, 14.214; 2nd, 8.655; 3rd, 5.369; top, 3.901; reverse, 18.588:1; hypoid bevel final drive, 3.909:1 ratio. Road speed at 1000 r.p.m. in top gear, 17.9 m.p.h.
SUSPENSION: Front independent, by coil springs and wishbones; semi-elliptics at rear; hydraulic shock-absorbers all round.
STEERING: Rack-and-pinion; 3 turns lock-to-lock, 32ft. turning circle.
WHEELS: Centre-lock, knock-on wire wheels with tubed 5.60 by 14in. tyres.
BRAKES: Lockheed hydraulic; 10½in. discs at front, 10in. drums at rear; total swept area, 350 sq. in.
CONSTRUCTION: Unitary.
DIMENSIONS: Wheelbase, 7ft. 7½in.; track, 4ft. 2in. front and rear; length 12ft. 9½in.; width 5ft. 2in., height (with hood up) 4ft. 1¼in.; ground clearance 5in.
KERB WEIGHT: 18½cwt.
FUEL TANK: 10 gallons.

PERFORMANCE ON TEST

CONDITIONS: Mostly wet; cold, no wind; two occupants, premium fuel.
MAXIMUM SPEED: 105.6 m.p.h.
STANDING quarter-mile: 18.4s.
MAXIMUM in indirect gears (to 6000 r.p.m.): 1st, 29.5 m.p.h.; 2nd, 48.0; 3rd, 78.0.
ACCELERATION from rest through gears: 0-30, 3.8s.; 0-40, 5.8s.; 0-50, 8.2s.; 0-60, 12.0s.; 0-70, 16.2s.; 0-80, 22.5s.; 0-90, 32.8s.
ACCELERATION in top (with third in brackets): 20-40, 7.5s. (5.0); 30-50, 7.4s. (5.2); 40-60, 8.0s. (6.8); 50-70 9.6s. (7.8); 60-80, 15.8s.; 70-90, 17.0s.
BRAKING: 29ft. 8in. to stop from 30 m.p.h. in neutral.
FUEL CONSUMPTION: 23.8 m.p.g. on test; 27.4 on normal running.
SPEEDOMETER: 2 m.p.h. fast at 30 m.p.h.; 5 m.p.h fast at 100 m.p.h.

PRICE: £1365 including tax

It enables the car to respond to your every mood: pottering along quietly and easily in top at low speeds; tractable as any town-bred saloon in city traffic, yet quickly overtaking most traffic when up-changes are made at around 3500 revs; or really stepping it out if you push the rev-counter needle up into the 5500-6000 region.

Acceleration from standstill is only fractionally quicker than that of the superseded MG A Mark II — but then the bigger, beefier new motor doesn't have to work so hard to achieve this result.

It is obviously detuned, as the 11 percent increase in capacity gives only about 5 percent more power,

MODERN MOTOR — August 1963

helping to explain the smoother, quieter performance of the larger engine. At around 3000 r.p.m., torque increase is 17 percent.

At touring speeds the engine has a deeper, throatier rumble than any previous B.M.C. unit I can remember. At over 4000 revs, this note changes to a harder pitch.

Top-gear acceleration from slow speeds is one of the few "un-MG-like" features, being more in the "Dynaflash Fireball 8" class. Top-gear hill-climbing power can also be likened to the "D.F.8."

Our 1-in-4 test hill was tackled at 15 m.p.h. in second from the base. Accelerating all the way up, we crested the top at 45 m.p.h. — still accelerating. I was too amazed to think about changing up to third.

Fuel economy is in direct relation to the amount of lead contained in your right boot. Genteel motoring rewarded us with 27.4 m.p.g. — but high-speed tests naturally put a severe strain on fuel economy, reducing the overall figure to 23.8.

Since the MG B is a sports car, the 10-gallon fuel tank is a happy compromise, giving a reasonable range of about 250 miles (even with a fair proportion of high-spirited pedalling) without adding too much weight.

True MG Handling

With such big changes in construction and styling, I had expected to find some differences in behavior. Not so — ride and handling appear to be almost unchanged.

This is both a vice and a virtue. After 50 miles or so you realise the suspension is definitely "firm" —

yet it is this very firmness which gives the MG its sensitivity, allowing the driver to "feel" just what the car is doing in relation to the road surface.

Steering characteristic is still very definitely toward oversteer. But not at full chat on a good highway, where fast curves can be taken in a smooth arc — under these conditions steering is almost neutral.

It's on the tighter corners, where the lower cogs are hurriedly grabbed, that the old MG oversteer becomes evident. Altering tyre pressures made little difference.

On wet road surfaces, the steeper corners were, to put it mildly, excitingly "hairy" if taken with any gusto. However, steering correction alone (without applying extra power) was usually enough to straighten things out. Body roll was almost nonexistent.

Steering ratio is a fraction slower than on the MG A; all the better for it, and reassuringly responsive in front-wheel turning action — but I wish the steering wheel wasn't so stiff to turn in the column. It robs the system of much sensitivity.

Cockpit, Controls

This must be the first MG sports whose cockpit gives a feeling of spacious comfort, wooing you with attractively upholstered, comfortable seats, full-width carpeting, wind-up windows, a neatly cowled, fully-instrumented dash panel — even a lockable glovebox.

An improvement was noted in the gearbox synchro, the changes being noticeably smoother and easier. The shift lever is nicely positioned and just the right length to afford good

leverage, so you don't finish up with a sore palm after a day's motoring.

Thanks to the new chassisless construction, the pedal controls are no longer crammed together; but the accelerator is small, and set so far from the brake pedal that heel-and-toeing is almost impossible. An organ pedal would solve this problem.

It was also surprising to find a normal ratchet-type handbrake lever (positioned between driver's seat and transmission tunnel) instead of the traditional "fly-off" type. However, it proved eminently satisfactory, holding the car on one of the steeper pinches of the Silverdale hillclimb course.

The disc/drum footbrake layout worked like a charm. Despite the absence of a power booster, it called for moderate pedal pressure and stopped us in less than 30ft. from 30 m.p.h. in neutral. Braking was progressive, free from squeal and fade-free.

Disappointingly, the boot is only slightly roomier than the MG A's. If the spare wheel could be carried elsewhere, boot space would be vastly improved — but I can think of no more practical spot for it than right where it is: in a lockable boot.

The MG B cannot hope to please every sports-car enthusiast, but I'm willing to bet it will please the vast majority. It IS a genuine sports car, despite its "roadster" appearance, and it DOES have a true everyday usefulness — unlike many so-called sports cars you see transported to race meetings on trailers.

To this everyday usefulness you can add bags of performance, with refinement, comfort and economy thrown in for good measure. Fair value at £1365, I calls it. ● ● ●

MG midget
what's in a name?

FIRST impressions CAN be misleading. Last month when we had a brief exploratory run in BMC's new baby MG — the Midget — we weren't too impressed.

We felt then that it had a vintage feel about it — almost as if it was a reincarnation of some earlier MG. The steering wheel is too big, and too close to the operator's chest, the ride is overly firm, without the suppleness we've come to expect of modern sportscars, and the handling was, to say the least, most unsporty.

None of these things have changed. But after spending a week with ESK 290, we find them not nearly as hard to live with as we had imagined they would be.

What wasn't obvious when we first drove the car was the tremendous revvability of the motor, and the quite good performance it offered. With only a few miles up the car was of course very stiff, and completely lacking in the flexibility we found so enjoyable when we drove it later.

What's new?

Basically, the Midget is just the Austin Healey Sprite with the name changed. BMC found that the magic of the octagonal MG nameplate was attracting buyers — the MGB is the country's best-selling sports-car, despite a price tag considerably in excess of the Sprite, Honda and Spitfire.

So they did the obvious thing, phasing out the Sprite in the second half of 1967 and introducing the MG Midget in early 1968.

Most important single difference between the two cars lies in the engine compartment. The Sprite used a tuned 1098 cc. motor and it produced 59 bhp at 5750 rpm and 65 lb. ft. of torque at 3500 rpm.

The Midget uses a 1275 cc. motor — basically the Mini Cooper S unit but detuned to the extent of smaller valves and a milder camshaft — which produces 65 bhp at 6000 rpm and 72 lb. ft. of torque at 3000 rpm. Compression ratio is slightly down from 8.9 to 8.8 to 1.

The Sprite was never a difficult car to drive in traffic. It's light weight and the flexibility of the 1100 motor were sufficient to allow it to potter along with the best of the family sedans. Imagine then how much better the Midget is with considerably more torque developed at lower rpm.

It's a great potterer — at the same time having a good reserve of performance on tap, irrespective of the gear ratio used.

Speaking of gear ratios brings us to a piece of news that will definitely interest potential Midget buyers. If they haven't already done so, BMC will shortly fit synchromesh to first gear.

That will be an improvement, although we never had difficulty engaging first on the move — either by double declutching, or just gritting our teeth and crunching it in.

Part of the Midget's flexibility is no doubt due to a final drive ratio which many critics feel is too low. The Midget's tachometer is red-lined at 6300 rpm but the 4.22 final drive ratio allows the car to run to 7000 rpm in top without any trouble at all. That gives it an outright top speed of 107 mph — because it is geared to do 15.5 mph/1000 rpm.

We did the right thing though and backed-off the throttle on our top speed runs, going through the traps with the tacho on the red line. This gave us 93.7 mph in both directions.

If you chose to ignore the red line, the Midget's top speed is a fair and square 107. Incidentally, BMC say the motor is capable of standing 7000 rpm without breaking to pieces.

Appointments

Like the Sprite that's gone before, the Midget offers pretty reasonable comfort for two people.

The seats are pleasant to sit on — more so, we think, than the Sprite's — although they look the same. They don't provide that hip-hugging support essential for ultimate comfort at speed, but by wedging oneself against the door and seatback and belting up with the standard seatbelt it is possible to stay firmly located.

The cabin area is fully carpeted, and a handy shelf behind the rear seats is also nicely trimmed with carpet. A good feature of this shelf area is that it is not made completely useless when

Sprite replacement turns out a much better car than we had at first expected

MODERN MOTOR — FEBRUARY 1968

MG
midget

e hood is stowed. With the top down, ere is still room for a considerable mount of soft luggage in addition to at area provided in the miniscule oot.

The Midget's hood is a considerable finement over the Sprite's — not so uch in the mechanics of erecting and wering as in mode of stowage.

Once it is folded up, it can be neatly dden under a half tonneau — and, we've already said, it doesn't riously interfere with stowage.

Visibility is not brilliant in any direcon, but this is not unusual in sportsrs. The windscreen is rather low, d the mini wipers sweep only a small ea.

Handling, brakes

The Midget is a very strong undereerer, and while we appreciate that is feature makes it a safe vehicle r the young and somewhat inperienced drivers who will buy it, it not the least sporty.

The color action pictures of the MG ow BMC rally ace Evan Green at the eel. Despite his considerable skill d daring, he just wasn't able to duce a tail-out oversteer attitude at y stage of our photographic sesons, and he tried handbrake turns d all!

We subsequently pumped the front res (Dunlop SP41 radials are standard) up to 30 psi and this reduced the dersteer quite a bit.

On dirt roads, of course, the tail ngs out. Acceleration on loose surces causes the rigid rear axle to amp and dither, and on very rough ctions the front tyres chafe on the eel arches.

Steering is rack and pinion, and very direct at 2.3 turns lock to lock. Sharp and sensitive on good surfaces, it produces a lot of feedback and chatter on poor roads. A touch more self-centring would help, too.

One of the Midget's most outstanding features is its superb braking ability. It is one of only two cars we've so far subjected to our crash braking test that has recorded a full 1g stop. And it did this not once but twice in succession. See our performance panel for more details.

The Dunlops SP41s, which have a legendary reputation for stickiness, are obviously contributing considerably to the Midget's braking.

Performance

We've already talked at some length about the Midget's top speed. Acceleration is most respectable. The car ran a best S.S. ¼-mile of 18.8 sec. and averaged 18.9, and accelerated to 60 in 12.5 sec.

Mid-range acceleration is good. The car's flexibility is such that it will run along on a whiff of throttle and take off strongly when the throttle is opened.

The average owner could expect 33-34 mpg. We achieved this in our normal running around, dropped the consumption to 27 when we did our performance runs. The six-gallon fuel tank is totally inadequate.

There's nothing really new about the MG Midget except the name — it's a collection of bits with which we're all pretty familiar. However, it's a mixture that blends well, and one that is easy to like.

We like it — despite our earlier misgivings. We're sure young sports-car enthusiasts will like it, too. ●

Manufacturer: BMC (Aust.) Pty. Ltd., Zetland, Sydney.
Test car supplied by them.
Price as tested: $2480.

SPECIFICATIONS

ENGINE
Water cooled, four cylinders in line, cast iron block, three main bearings.
Bore x stroke .... 70.6 x 81.2 mm.
Capacity .... 1275 cc. (77.9 cu. in.)
Compression .... 8.8 to 1
Carburettor .... Twin SUs
Fuel pump .... Electrical
Fuel tank .... 6 gallons
Fuel recommended .... super
Valve gear .... pushrod ohv
Max. power (gross) .... 65 bhp at 6000 rpm
Max. torque .... 72 lb./ft. at 3000 rpm
Specific power-output .... 51 bhp/litre
Electrical system .... 12v, 43 amp hr. battery

TRANSMISSION
Four-speed manual with synchro on upper three ratios. Single dry plate clutch.

Gear	Ratio	Mph/1000 rpm	Max. mph
1st	3.2	5.0	30 (6000)
2nd	1.916	8.3	50 (6000)
3rd	1.357	11.6	70 (6000)
4th	1.00	15.5	98 (6300)
Final drive ratio			4.22 to 1

CHASSIS
Wheelbase .... 6ft. 8in.
Track front .... 3ft. 10¾in.
Track rear .... 3ft. 8¼in.
Length .... 11ft. 5in.
Width .... 4ft. 6¼in.
Height .... 4ft. 1in.
Clearance .... 5in.
Kerb weight .... 14 cwt. 35 lb.
Weight distribution front/rear ... 52.4/47.6%

SUSPENSION
Front: Independent by coils and wishbones, with tubular shock absorbers.
Rear: Rigid axle with semi-elliptic leaf springs and tubular shock absorbers.
Brakes: 8¼in. disc, 7in. drum. 190 sq. in. of swept area.
Steering .... Rack and pinion
Turns lock to lock 2.1/3
Turning circle .... 32ft.
Wheels: Knock-off wire with 5.20 by 13 tubeless radial tyres.

PERFORMANCE

Top speed .... 94.1 mph
Average (both ways) .... 93.7 mph
Standing quarter-mile .... 18.9 sec.

Acceleration

Zero to		seconds
30 mph		3.7
40 mph		6.0
50 mph		9.0
60 mph		12.5
70 mph		16.5
80 mph		25.1

	3rd	top
20-40 mph	5.7	—
30-50 mph	5.5	8.0
40-60 mph	6.3	7.4
50-70 mph	6.7	7.7

BRAKING: Ten crash stops from 60 mph.

Stop	percent G	pedal pressure
1	95	80 lb.
2	100	90 lb.
3	100	100 lb.
4	95	95 lb.
5	95	95 lb.
6	95	100 lb.
7	90	105 lb.
8	85	110 lb.
9	80	110 lb.
10	80	120 lb.

Comments: Rear brake lock-up on stops 4 and 5.
Consumption: 27 mpg over 112 miles, including all tests; 34.1 mpg in normal country and suburban use.

Speedo error:

Indicated mph	30	40	50	60	70	80
Actual mph	28.1	37.8	47.4	56.4	66.1	75.2

MGB
MARK 2

FIRST acquaintance with the Mark 2 MGB recently led us to believe that nothing much had changed since we last drove the car about four years ago.

Obvious things — like the driving position and pedal arrangement—are pretty much as we remembered — and they leave something to be desired.

In certain aspects of equippage, too, the new car falls short of its predecessor. For instance, there is less cockpit carpeting than there used to be.

It's not until you get the car out on the road and stir it along that the differences between the Mark 2 and earlier MGBs become obvious. BMC are making much of a new, all-synchro gearbox and electric overdrive and these things are, sure enough, notable improvements.

But it is really the dozens of subtle changes hardly worthy of individual mention that make this car considerably more pleasant than previous Bs we've driven.

It is quieter, more rigid, more weatherproof, more responsive, more roadworthy and, in the ultimate, safer, and more fun.

Fun it might be. When you take a hard look at the car you also realise that it is something of a relic. It's ancestral ties with MG TDs, TFs, and MGAs are painfully obvious — through its dated rigid rear axle, its rack and pinion steering with so much castor action that self-centring is virtually non-existent, its jarring ride on poor surfaces, its giant economy-size steer-ing wheel, its stuffy, badly ventilated cabin, and its awkward collapsing hood.

Today, young motorists with $3500 or thereabouts to spend on a motor car (the B retails at $3325) can choose between Holden GTS, Alfa T1, BMW 1600, Volvo 122S, etc.

Despite such tempting alternatives, the MGB continues to perform well in the market place. It is Australia's biggest - selling sportscar, accounting for about 50 percent of total sales. However, sports cars account for a shrinking percentage of the overall market, as more and more people switch to the various alternatives already mentioned.

If we take this development to its logical conclusion we can assume that the days of the MGB are numbered.

BMC probably realise this, and that why there have been no sweeping revisions to its specifications.

(If there was a revision, we hope would be along the lines of the curent MGB GT coupe, but with t aluminium Rover V8 engine, and all-independent rear end.)

In the meantime about 1200 enthusiasts (most of them young) a buying MGBs every year. They're buing a sports car with good handlin firm (too firm) ride, precise steerin excellent brakes, acceptable comfo and pleasant looks.

Specifications

The engine uses the B series BM block which is fitted to the Aust 1800 as well. Like the 1800 the dimesions are undersquare at 80.26 mr

There's life in this old girl, yet!
Recent modifications have given
the hoary MGB a new lease on life

ore by 88.9 mm. stroke for a cubic
apacity of 1798 cc.

Compression ratio is 8.8 to 1, and
he engine develops 95 bhp at 5400
om and 110 lb. ft. of torque at 3000
om.

Twin SU HS4 carburettors are fitted.

New on the Mark 2 motor is an
lternator. The gearbox is, as we've al-
eady pointed out, revised. It has
ynchromesh on first gear now, and
he ratios have been rearranged to
ive a better spread. First will run to
2 mph, second to 50, third to 75.
When the new overdrive is flicked in,
hird (o/d) runs to 90. Straight top
ives a ton, while overdrive top will
un to about 107 mph.

Notchy box

In operation the box is consider-
ble improved. It still has that notchy
eel typical of all MGs, but slot selec-
ion is easier, especially if the clutch
edal is pressed right to the floor.

Suspension is dead conventional—
oils and wishbones at the front, with
a live axle and semi-elliptics at the
ear. However, spring, shock absorber
nd roll bar settings have been revised
with the result that the Mark 2 rolls
nore, but rides ever-so-slightly softer
han the earlier car.

Steering is rack and pinion, very
direct with 2.9 turns lock to lock, and
with practically no self-centring action.

This is disconcerting and takes a
ittle getting used to. The Mark 2's
steering behavior is tremendously

MGB MARK 2

improved over earlier Bs though, by the simple addition of radial ply tyres which are now standard equipment.

Understeer is minimised at speeds up to 70 mph, and only becomes evident above that.

The steering otherwise is pin sharp, very responsive, and informative to the driver.

It is spoiled to a great extent by an enormous, old-fashioned steering wheel. BMC in Sydney, realising this, fitted a smaller, leather-bound wheel to one of their test cars and the difference in controllability and comfort between the two was enormous.

Brakes are very good. MG was one of the very first to fit a front disc/rear drum braking arrangement back in the days when the MGA was all the rage with young bloods.

The MGB continues to offer excellent braking power. The system doesn't have servo assistance, yet pedal pressures are quite light, and the action of the brakes progressive and controllable.

Comfort

For a sports car, the B offers quite acceptable comfort. The seats are pleasantly soft yet provide good lateral, lumbar and under-thigh support.

The collapsing hood seems even snugger on the Mark 2, but it still isn't

a piece of cake to erect or disassemble. If you were caught in a summer downpour in Sydney, you'd be well-and-truly saturated by the time you got the top up.

Once it is in place, however, it provides draft-free ventilation, and doesn't leak, even in a summer downpour.

Performance

The MGB is not really a ball of fire. It will be "hosed off" at traffic lights by V8 Holdens and Falcons, Mini Coopers, Datsun 2000s, etc., etc., with some ease. It is, however, the most accelerative stock MG we've ever driven. We managed one standing-quarter in 17.7 sec. which proved exceptional. Others were all in the 18.0-18.2 region.

Ninety mph is reached in 31 sec. and, thanks to the overdrive, which provides an effortless 22 mph/1000 rpm, this speed can be maintained easily as long as the road allows.

The standard muffling is sufficiently quiet to be non-tiring at these speeds, although the hood roars considerably in the upper speed brackets, and there is a lot of mechanical noise. From about 70 mph onwards the radio fitted to the test car was difficult to hear.

The B handles very precisely, the standard equipment radial tyres (Olympic GTs they were) providing excellent adhesion in both wet and dry.

On rough surfaces, ride is very harsh, although the car feels more rigid than any MG we've driven previously. The few rattles that appeared all seemed to be in the hood, and there was very little "scuttle shake", an old sports car bogey.

On loose surfaces, the B can be induced to hang its tail out readily. It

does so with a great deal of decorum and remains perfectly controllable, no matter how outlandish the attitude.

Thanks to that overdrive, the B can be toured at high speed with outstanding economy. A figure of 30 mp was achieved on one rapid country trip although our test procedure, over course of 262 miles, returned 26 mp.

While on that subject we think would be an improvement if the over drive control were relocated for use with the left (or gearchanging) hand.

In its present location on the extreme right of the dash, running through the six gears in acceleration requires some fancy hand movement — and until the driver become thoroughly acquainted, considerab concentration.

Safety

Among the many refinements included on the Mark 2 are some designed to minimise injury for occupants. The window winders and door handles are crushable or recessed. The eared, "knock-off" wheel hub have been dispensed with in favor of giant octagonal locking nuts, also for safety purposes, and seat belts are standard equipment.

Other improvements include reversing lights, a laminated windscreen and a headlamp flasher.

Not so much a safety item as insurance against expensive engine damage is the oil cooler which is now standard.

All these things serve to make the MGB a better, more complete package Despite its flaws, it is still a car which is fun to drive, and that, after all, is the name of the game.

MODERN MOTOR — MARCH 196

DATA SHEET— MGB MARK 2

Manufacturer: BMC (Aust.) Pty. Ltd.

Test car supplied by them.

Price as tested: $3325.

SPECIFICATIONS

ENGINE

Water-cooled, four cylinders in line, cast iron block, five main bearings.

Bore x stroke	80.26 x 88.9 mm.
Capacity	1798 cc.
Compression	8.8 to 1
Carburettors	twin SU HS4
Fuel pump	electrical
Fuel tank	12 gallons
Fuel recommended	super
Valve gear	pushrod ohv
Max. power (gross)	95 bhp at 5400 rpm
Max. torque	110 lb. ft. at 3000 rpm
Specific power output	54.5 bhp/litre
Electrical system	12v, 58 amp hr. battery, 15 AC alternator

TRANSMISSION

Four-speed manual all-synchro gearbox, with electric overdrive on third and top. Single dry-plate clutch.

Gear	Ratio	Overall	Mph/1000 rpm
Rev.	4.755	18.577	—
1st	3.440	13.446	—
2nd	2.160	8.470	—
3rd	1.380	5.394	—
4th	1.000	3.909	17.9
4th o/d	0.802	3.200	22.0
Final drive ratio		3.909 to 1	

CHASSIS

Wheelbase	8ft 7in.
Track front	4ft. 1in.
Track rear	4ft. 1¼in.
Length	12ft. 9in.
Width	5ft.
Height	4ft. 1¼in.
Clearance	5in.
Kerb weight	17 cwt. 70 lb.
Weight distribution front/rear	54/46%
lb/bhp	20.1 lb.

SUSPENSION

Front: Independent by coils and wishbones, stabiliser bar, telescopic shock absorbers.

Rear: Live axle, with semi-elliptic leaf springs, telescopic shock absorbers.

Brakes: Disc/drum, 310 sq. in. of swept area.

Steering	rack and pinion
Turns lock to lock	2.9
Turning circle	32ft.

Wheels: Knock-off wire with 165 by 14 tubed radial tyres.

PERFORMANCE

Top speed	107 mph
Average (both ways)	105 mph
Standing quarter-mile	18.0 sec.

Acceleration

Zero to	sec.
30 mph	4.1
40 mph	5.4
50 mph	8.0
60 mph	11.1
70 mph	15.0
80 mph	20.9
90 mph	31.1

	3rd	top
20-40 mph	5.3	—
30-50 mph	5.1	7.9
40-60 mph	5.7	7.8
50-70 mph	6.4	8.1
60-80 mph	—	9.7

BRAKING: Five crash stops from 60 mph.

Stop	percent G	pedal pressure
1	.89	56 lb.
2	.90	55 lb.
3	.87	58 lb.
4	.82	60 lb.
5	.81	60 lb.

Consumption: 26 mpg over 262 miles, including all tests; 30 mpg in normal country and suburban use.

Speedo error:

Indicated mph	30	40	50	60	70
Actual mph	28.5	37.8	47.7	56.8	65.4

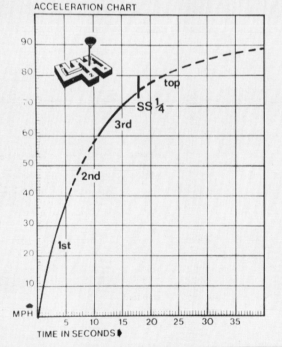

ACCELERATION CHART

(vertical axis: MPH 10 to 90; horizontal axis: TIME IN SECONDS 5 to 35)

1st, 2nd, 3rd, SS ¼, top

HOW MGB MARK 2 COMPARES

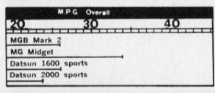

MAXIMUM SPEED (mean) M.P.H.

	80	90	100	110	120
MGB Mark 2 ($3325)					
MG Midget ($2554)					
Datsun 1600 sports ($3049)					
Datsun 2000 sports ($3509)					

0-60 M.P.H. SECONDS

	25	15	5
MGB Mark 2			
MG Midget			
Datsun 1600 sports			
Datsun 2000 sports			

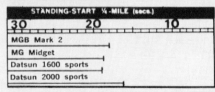

M.P.G. Overall

	20	30	40
MGB Mark 2			
MG Midget			
Datsun 1600 sports			
Datsun 2000 sports			

STANDING-START ¼-MILE (secs.)

	30	20	10
MGB Mark 2			
MG Midget			
Datsun 1600 sports			
Datsun 2000 sports			

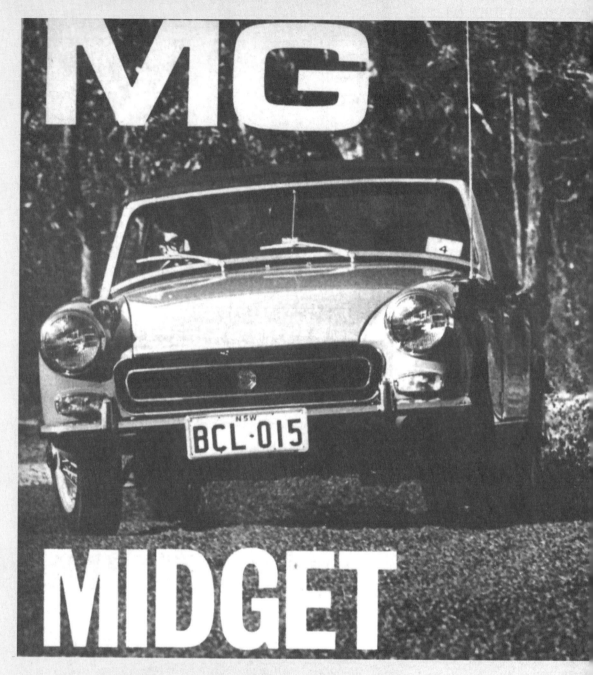

MG

MIDGET

Detail improvements and a "mod" paint job give the MG Midget a new lease of life — even if the concept is outdated

THE MG Midget makes a great road test car. You pick it up on a Friday, enjoy a sunny weekend with the fast-folding hood down, then hand it back on Monday morning.

Past that, its practical limitations will try even the tolerance of the "young-at-heart".

It is a tremendous fun car, is great to learn about real "driving" and relishes an aggressive technique.

But to own, it needs to be a fourth car for when the mood suits or a bachelor-catcher town commuter for the career girl. Alternatively, it form basis of great potential for the serio club motor sport aficionado.

We handed the keys back to t British Leyland after a 300-mile t having loved every moment in t endearing little roadster, but qu happy to step out.

The latest version, the Midget M Two has been updated to ke in-vogue with the "seventies swingers New grille and rear bumpere treatment plus a blac chrome-stripped sill section re-juvena

...e basic "Spridget" body introduced ...even years ago, as the second series ...ustin-Healey Sprite.

Apart from the dress pizzazz and ...dditional safety gear, the Mark Two ...Midget differs in only one mechanical ...ecification — the rear axle ratio. But ...his seemingly innocuous item has ...ansformed the small sporty. In our ...oad-test of the first Australian Midget ...n Modern Motor, February 1968 we ...ommented how the car needed a ...taller" final drive. And that is what ...ritish-Leyland has given the Mark ...wo — uprated on numerical values ...rom 4.222 to 3.9 to 1.

Theorists would tell you that will ...educe acceleration but increase top ...peed. In fact, and due to the Midget's ...ow-tune 1275 cc Morris Cooper ...ngine, the tremendous torque keeps ...cceleration up and also gives higher ...peed in all gears.

We saw 6250 (start of the red tacho ...ector) in the indirect gears and 5500 ...pm in top — equivalent to 101 mph, ...nd increase of seven mph over the ...222 to 1-geared Midget.

...mproved handling

The revised gearing which gives ...naxima of 35, 60 and 86, has the ...ndirect benefit of transforming the ...andling also. Because the car is on ...eak torque at higher speeds, it is easy ...o flick around in a most controlled ...vay. There is still pronounced initial ...ndersteer but a strong prod of the ...ccelerator lets the enterprising driver ...se power oversteer where he wants. ...The direct, if stiff steering (the test ...ar had 4000 miles up and the steering ...till seemed "sticky") and excellent ...ontrol ergonomics — gearshift, pedal ...ocation and brakes — give a feeling of ...nastery and confidence. It is easy to ...ee why the Midget wears such a high ...nsurance loading as the less ...xperienced driver would exploit this ...onfidence too far.

Perhaps the only handling vice comes ...rom the quite low ratio of track to ...vheelbase size and soft springing ...vhich makes the car "dive" noticeably ...vhile cornering on a trailing throttle. ...This roll oversteer can be used ...uccessfully to "set-up", the Midget ...or tight cornering, especially on ...oanked turns where the tail will lean ...nto the banking in an oversteer ...ttitude without really needing ...pposite lock. Used this way the ...Vlidget's handling is a real delight with ...he car showing magic response.

Less endearing is the trait of engine ...orque reflex. Driving on a straight ...oad, the Midget will alter course ...ramatically with throttle movement. ...Hard acceleration to trailing throttle ...wings the nose left, trailing to ...ower-on a less dramatic pull to the ...ight. Although the suspension is to ...ports cars standards, it is quite soft ...vhich allows the torque reflex such ...dvantage.

But over dirt roads, the suspension ...vins and you can forget most of that bone-jarring-sports-car-ride idea. The back axle is sufficiently well located to handle even the worst corrugations

The front — on coils and double lever action shockers — is supple enough to keep directional stability high. We can now see why John Sprinzel put up such a good show in the London-to-Sydney Marathon when all critics decried the baby, over-laden Midget as a toy. Up to Broken Hill on the third last day Sprinzel lay first private entrant outright before he broke a front stub axle. Despite its diminutive size, the body cross-members and sub-frames make the Midget a solid, rattle-free car.

Whilst the Midget could not be taken too seriously — except as extreme personalised transport for those prepared to accept its crudities — it is an uncompromising sports car.

And the 1970 definition of a sports car is a ragtop — for there are many sedans for the same money which will match the Midget in performance, braking and even handling.

New fittings

But no sedan can offer a one-handed drop top, without even climbing out. That's one of the strong features carried over from the last Midget model. The top comes down by flipping two catches, undoing some press-studs and folding the steel-framed hood back behind the seats. It is neat, simple and easy-to-use.

An anti-roll bar, multi-laced wire wheels and oil cooler are UK market, extra-cost options which come in the Australian ckd packs as standard.

These combine with the 1970 additions of vinyl-bound, alloy-spoked steering wheel, reclining seats, laminated windscreen and radial ply tyres to up-date the Midget. Twin reversing lights, a combined flasher/dip switch, indicators, horn stalk, a fresh-air heater and new thicker carpets make the Midget more livable and comfortable.

British-Leyland even says the Midget is quieter but we'd dispute that. At peak rpm in third, the mechanical wail announces the Midget's flight several miles back. There is less gearbox noise in this model but first is still un-synchronised and screeches the familiar Morris whine under a heavy right foot.

Despite the noise, the new Midget does seem more accommodating. The test car was not fitted with a heater, only a fresh air plenum chamber with dash control for side flaps into the foot-wells. It is a lucky dip whether you get the billed-as-standard-equipment heater, as they are omitted from some ckd kits. Even with the hood down, night travel would be cosy with this addition. We found, with no heater the cockpit warmed-up from engine and transmission heat — eventually.

While the new flasher stalk is better ergonomically than the floor dipper, it is stiff and hard to use. Other switch gear also is lacking pre-thought on easy operation. The wiper and washer controls live on the far left which would be great for lhd cars but calls for hands off the wheel on rhd cars. As the dash is so close, the all important wipers and washers could be at finger-reach.

The US export car gets three-blade wipers. Why, British Leyland, do we not get them here with twin-speed motors and power washers? At $2670, crying "cost" is not justification.

For those who like the Midget but not its wind-in-the-hair there is an optional hardtop which makes the cockpit cosier but defeats much of the aim of this low-cost drop-head.

The little Midget commands considerable respect as a serious attempt to build a not-so-serious car. It is tight and safe for the clientele it will attract. But it is not very good value and with the tremendous insurance loadings it attracts there will be little change from $3000 once you've put the car on the road with all accessories, registration and insurance.

If you can put up with the crudities, looking down the barrel of diesel bus exhausts, being spattered with mud and slush on wet days and not being able to see around that Mini in front, then the Midget will soon start winning you. Certainly, outside city smog, it has to be a groovy way to get your favourite bird to the beach.

But, like we said, it was no struggle giving it back when the time came. ●

DATA SHEET— MG MIDGET

Manufacturer: BLMC (Aust.) Pty. Ltd.
Test car supplied by: BLMC, Zetland, NSW.
Price as tested: $2670

ENGINE

Water cooled, 4 cylinders in line. Cast iron block, 3 main bearings.

Bore x stroke	70.6 x 81.2mm
Capacity	1275cc
Compression	8.8 to 1
Carburettor	twin SUs
Fuel pump	electrical
Fuel tank	6 gallons
Fuel recommended	super
Valve gear	p'rod ohv
Max. power (gross)	65 bhp at 6000 rpm
Max. torque	72 lb. ft. at 3000 rpm
Specific power output	51 bhp/litre
Electrical system	12v, 43 amp hr battery, at 20-hr rate, alternator.

TRANSMISSION

Four speed manual, with synchro on upper three ratios. Single dry plate clutch.

Gear	Ratio	Mph/1000 Rpm	Max. mph	
Rev.	4.100	4.5	28	6250
1st	3.200	5.8	36	6250
2nd	1.916	9.6	60	6250
3rd	1.357	13.6	85	6250
4th	1.000	18.5	102	5500

Final drive ratio .... 3.9 to 1

CHASSIS

Wheelbase	6ft. 8in.
Track front	3ft. 10¼in.
Track rear	3ft. 8¾in.
Length	11ft. 5in.
Width	4ft. 6½in.
Height	4ft. 1in.
Clearance	5in.
Kerb weight	14 cwt. 35lbs.
Weight distribution front/rear	52/48 percent
lb/bhp	29.5

SUSPENSION

Front: Independent by wishbones, coil springs and lever-action hydraulic shock absorbers.
Rear: Rigid axle with semi-elliptic leaf springs and telescopic hydraulic shock absorbers.
Brakes: 8¼in disc, 7in. drum, 190 sq. in. of swept area.
Steering .... rack and pinion
Turns lock to lock 2 1/3
Turning circled .... 32ft. (av.)
Wheels: Knock-off wire with 145 by 13 tubed radial tyres.

PERFORMANCE

Top speed .... 102 mph
Average (both ways) .... 102 mph

Standing quarter mile .... 18.6 sec

Acceleration
Zero to .... seconds

30 mph		4.
40 mph		5.
50 mph		8.
60 mph		12.
70 mph		16.
80 mph		22.

	3rd	to
20-40 mph	6.0	8.
30-50 mph	5.6	9.
40-60 mph	6.0	9.
50-70 mph	7.9	10.

BRAKING: Five crash stops from 60 mph

Stop	percent G	pedal pressure
1	95	80
2	95	90
3	100	90
4	95	95
5	95	95

Consumption: 26 mpg over 114 mile including all tests; 32 mpg in normal country and suburban use.

Speedo error

Indicated mph	30	40	50	60	70	80
Actual mph	30	38	47	56	66	75

ACCELERATION CHART

TOP 4
3RD
SS¼
2ND
1ST

MPH / TIME IN SECONDS

HOW MG MIDGET COMPARES

MAXIMUM SPEED (mean) M.P.H.
MG Midget ($2670)
Toyota Corolla 1200 coupe ($2567)
Fiat 850S coupe ($2509)
Mazda R100 ($2835)

0-60 M.P.H. SECONDS
MG Midget
Toyota Corolla 1200 coupe
Fiat 850S coupe
Mazda R100

M.P.G. Overall
MG Midget
Toyota Corolla 1200 coupe
Fiat 850S coupe
Mazda R100

STANDING START ¼ MILE (secs)
MG Midget
Toyota Corolla 1200 coupe
Fiat 850S coupe
Mazda R100